T H E
SIXTIES

A PICTORIAL REVIEW

THE
SiXTiEs

A PICTORIAL REVIEW

Chris Pearce

BLOSSOM

An H. C. Blossom Book

Copyright © H. C. Blossom

A catalogue record for this book is available from the British Library

ISBN 1 872532 27 6

Design: Jacquie Burgess and Ivor Claydon

Typeset in Great Britain by SX Composing, Rayleigh, Essex.

Printed and bound in Hong Kong

H. C. Blossom
6/7 Warren Mews
London W1P 5DJ

CONTENTS

INTRODUCTION

The landing of the first man on the moon was the fulfilment of an ancient human dream as well as a momentous technological achievement — some may have regarded it as a potential turning-point in man's cosmic consciousness — but the mood of the sixties meant that it was generally seen at best as a distraction, more commonly as an irrelevant extravagance. The world had grown out of the simplistic ambitions it had inherited from the fifties, and it didn't take an astronaut's poignant description to make it aware of its vulnerability. Television, which in the early sixties had brought an immediacy to such events as the Cuban crisis, the deaths of Kennedy and Oswald and (on a lighter note) the arrival of the first media-wise pop group, the Beatles, ensured that the moonshot was seen against the ever-present backdrop of famine, war and civil injustice: against Biafra, Vietnam, Czechoslovakia, Northern Ireland, civil rights issues and the early stages of the ecology movement. In this context it had to be judged as a magnificent anachronism.

The unique contribution of the sixties to social history was the concept of the *global village* — a legacy which might be seen as vindicating the decade. For whereas the fifties can be seen as pushing the doctrines of consumerism to extremes, so the sixties were a laboratory of human behaviour.

Beatlemania reached an hysterical crescendo when it hit the USA, reaching the cover of Life *magazine and bringing in its wake a British invasion of music and fashion.*

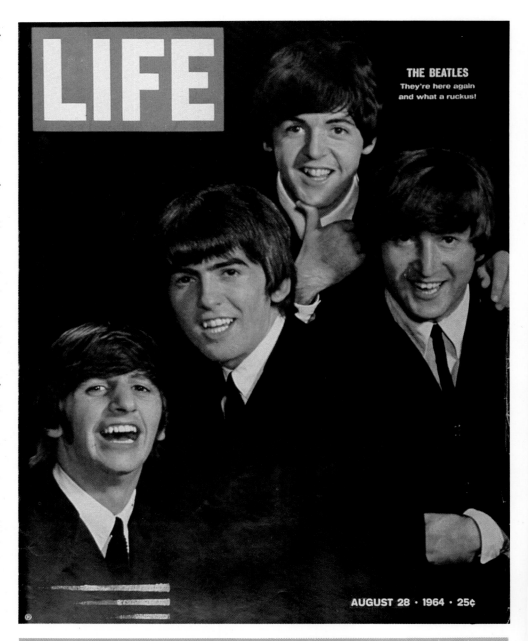

JULY 21ST 1969:

ONE SMALL STEP FOR A MAN,

ONE GIANT LEAP FOR MANKIND.

The space helmet style of the hairdryers is purely coincidental, of course. Even so, housewives were promised a new era of spin-off technological benefits from the space programme, including non-stick frying pans!

Kings Road Chelsea vied with Carnaby Street as the Mecca of the Mods, whilst the fashion revolution brought the boutique phenomenon to every high street.

*I*n June 1960 occurred one of those seemingly inconsequential events that from time to time sow the seeds of something quite momentous; a small Liverpool cellar jazz club announced the end of its strictly jazz-only policy. Henceforth, rock 'n' roll groups could appear on its tiny stage.

The beginning of the new decade saw a Britain still very much living in the past. Nevertheless, under the surface lurked various elements which would emerge – spontaneously, it seemed – at about the same time that The Cavern and its favourite sons, the Beatles, became the focal point of a new British empire. These elements combined to create the image of the age and the speed with which they fused into what became the Swinging Sixties is indicative of the breakdown of the social repression which had characterised much of the fifties. In many ways, Britain in the sixties was making up for lost time – coming to terms with a con-

sumer society and with the traumas of post-imperialism as experienced in the Suez Crisis, repudiating the traditional class system and its values and, above all, regaining in the process its creative energy. The playful spirit of the age was embodied in two cult items – the Mini car and the motor scooter. Both were products of the fifties, originating in a need for economic, convenient transport, but the sixties saw them take on new, youthful personae. Youth was the key to everything, and virtually every aspect of life – politics, architecture, the arts, education, even that venerable symbol of the Establishment, the BBC – seemed to capitulate under the onslaught of the baby boom generation. The impact of this explosion was artificially exaggerated by contemporary commentators and journalists who, in their desire to see everything as a new phenomenon, obscured the fact that, for example, Mary Quant's Bazaar had been in existence since

1955 and that John Stephen had begun to transform male fashion in his Carnaby Street Shop in 1957. Likewise, Pop Art had been going since the late forties and even the Beatles, minus Ringo, dated back to 1958. Nevertheless, there was a genuine climate for new opportunities, particularly as the widespread rejection of establishment values broke down the class barriers. Superficially, at least, the new Britain was now a meritocracy, with youth and talent being the only credentials required. The result was a reversal of the previous order, such that modern Eliza Doolittles, epitomised by Twiggy, found accents that would have previously been studiously neutralised now to be a positive advantage, to the point where, at one time, it seemed that a Liverpool or Cockney accent was a prerequisite of success.

The New York offices of CBS were decorated in 1966 in a style which reflected the international image of large corporations.

'. . . Matter o' fact, Oi were Lady Chatterley's lover . . .'

The change that came over many aspects of British life was not the sensational overnight event that contemporary comentators portrayed. For example, the election of the Labour government under Harold Wilson in 1964 was heralded as the overthrow of the Establishment as personified by the deposed Tory, Alexander Douglas-Home, and yet as long ago as 1959 the then Tory leader, Harold MacMillan, had stated 'I think the class war is now obsolete.' In 1960, much was made of the marriage of Princess Margaret to a commoner, the photographer, Anthony Armstrong-Jones, as symbolic of the end of Britain's traditional class system, yet in the same year the prosecutor, Mr Griffith-Jones, in the case of Penguin Books, on trial under an obscenity charge for publishing D.H. Lawrence's *Lady Chatterley's Lover*, could ask the jury, without irony, "... would you approve of your young sons, young daughters – because girls can read as well as boys – reading this book. Is it a book that you would have lying around in your own house? Is it a book that you would even wish your wife or your servants to read?"

It was noted that the jury seemed taken aback by this assumption that they would have servants, and contemporary commentators saw it as yet another example of how out of touch the Establishment was.

Opposite *Even traditional pomp and ceremony could not detract from the social significance of Princess Margaret marrying a 'commoner'.*

The traditional concept of hereditary privilege was also challenged. In 1960 Anthony Wedgwood Benn (now Tony Benn) became Viscount Stansgate on the death of his father. In 1961 he attempted to take his seat as an MP in the Commons but was barred because of his title. In 1963 the Peerage Act allowed him to renounce his title and become a commoner again. Within a few months, the Earl of Hume took the same path to enable him to take his place in the Commons as the new Tory Prime Minister.

Debunking the Establishment was a popular sport in early sixties Britain. The satirical review *Beyond the Fringe*, 1961, with its four young Oxbridge graduate stars – Jonathan Miller, Alan Bennett, Peter Cook and Dudley Moore – heralded a new era of political and social iconoclasm in the tradition of the eighteenth century writers and caricaturists. The first satirical nightclub, known as The Establishment, attacked sacred cows as entertainment, and satire was televised in the weekly review of current events, *That Was The Week That Was*, which started in 1962, while *Private Eye* magazine, founded the previous year, lampooned them in print. As opinion-formers, the young, educated satirists were a powerful force and can be regarded as partial creators of the image of the Establishment, setting it up for its overthrow. The established order was changing in other ways too. In 1960 National Service (conscription into the armed services) was finally ended and, with it, one manifestation of the hand of authority. The next year, oral contraception in the form of the Pill became available, heralding the Sexual Revolution.

As well as the fine art renaissance of new talent which was showcased in the Young Contemporaries exhibition in 1961 and which became the Pop Art movement of the sixties, and a revival of theatre and film, the beginning of the decade saw a change in pop culture. There was a challenge to the American dominance of pop which had characterised the fifties. Although American dance crazes like the Twist were popular, as was American pop music, Britain now had its own pop music industry.

Left *Although Oxbridge was associated with elitism and privilege,* Beyond the Fringe *heralded a move towards a more classless, anti-Establishment era.* (**clockwise** *Peter Cook, Jonathan Miller, Alan Bennett, Dudley Moore*).

Right That Was The Week That Was *provided a satirical commentary on current events.*

And to crown it all, they had style. Although the Mod look was already established, the Beatles endorsed it as the definitive image of the early sixties, as well as, for the first time, making British pop the leader of world style. Not only did this revitalize the country's textile industry (which was to credit the Beatles as saviours of corduroy, which had hitherto been seen as a utility fabric) but also contributed to the homogenising of society as the early Mod look became incorporated into men's fashions, and *The Avengers'* John Steed epitomised the sartorial elegance of Saville Row Mod. Although the enduring popular image of the Mod movement is of convoys of scooters, customized with banks of lamps and mirrors, the riders uniformed in fur-trimmed parkas, these were second generation. The original Mods were the Individualists who, although distinguished by elegant dress, were closely linked in philosophy with the Beat Movement. As the name implies, the individual, or at least the outward appearance of individualism, was the key to a dress code which eschewed commercial teenage fashion. Modernists (Mods) favoured a smart, Italian-derived look. The principal source was John Stephen's Carnaby Shop, at that time a little establishment in an obscure London Street, but in the search for novelty, shoes from theatrical suppliers and even deliberately selected items from old-fashioned tailors would feature.

Left *The Vespa scooter, sharp suit and 'pork pie' hat epitomized the Mod image.*

Right *The Mod cult catapulted Carnaby Street from obscurity into an international symbol of Swinging London.*

Above *John Stephen (far right), secure in his status as king of Carnaby Street and Mod fashion.*

Although the Beatles' appearance was, in part, due to Brian Epstein (the only manager to have claimed something 'bigger than Elvis' and to be proved right) who groomed them, tidying-up their notorious long hair and kitting them out in Pierre Cardin style collarless Mod jackets, the roots of their style were derived from the European existentialist movement. Their style mentor, Astrid Kirchener, did much to transform them from scruffy rock 'n' rollers, giving them their distinctive combed-forward fringed hair and, through her photography, an awareness of their own photogenic qualities. There were other elements of sub pop style, such as the use of leather, hitherto seen only in motorcycle jackets, but now featured in the 'kinky' look,

which became exemplified by Honor Blackman in *The Avengers* – leather coats, caps, jackets, trousers (as worn by Gene Vincent), waistcoats, ties. Boots replaced shoes and the Beatles popularised elastic-sided, high cuban-heeled flamenco-type footwear which, as with many clothes of the time, anticipated unisex.

The visual impact of the Beatles extended to every aspect of their image. Even on stage they were excitingly different and though tame compared with what was about to happen (no guitars smashed or rammed through speakers or set alight or played by the teeth), their raw energy, its roots in American rock 'n' roll, shamed the current emasculated pop scene. Everything about them on stage seemed different. Left-

handed McCartney, with his old-fashioned-looking viola-bodied Hofner bass, gave the three guitar lineup an asymmetric look and the Beatles held their guitars high on their chests rather than at the conventional hip level, so they looked like rock 'n' roll troubadours. This mannerism was imitated to such an extent that groups began to play guitars virtually under their chins.

Below *Bikers remained loyal to the macho rock 'n' roll image.*

As other Liverpool groups capitalized on the success of Mersey beat, claims were made for other regional sounds – Birmingham, Manchester and even, in the case of the Dave Clark Five, the London suburb of Tottenham. It all became rather spurious. Meanwhile, the popularity and, once the initial shock had passed, the general acceptability of the Beatles (who even performed for royalty) disenchanted many early followers, although 'Beatlemania' did not die. Fanned by the press and the new phenomenon of spin-off marketing (virtually anything with Beatle pictures would sell, resulting in thousands of items, including clothes, 'Beatle' wigs, toys and posters), it received a second burst of energy when, after unsuccessful attempts on the market through 1963, the Beatles hit the USA with 'I Want to Hold Your Hand', reaching the number one spot in January 1964, backed by a $50,000 publicity campaign and the endorsement of appearing on the Ed Sullivan show.

Now with every company, haunted by the spectre of Decca who had turned down the Beatles, prepared to sign up any cult group, the British pop scene was totally transformed. Decca redeemed themselves by gaining the Rolling Stones, who were seen as an alternative to the Beatles. Much of the supposed rivalry between the two groups was in the minds of their fans and the press, but their presence increased the market and musical viability of British pop, stimulating the scene into a position where it would dominte Western pop music through the decade. Above all, the Rolling Stones heralded the major sixties theme of protest. The Beatles, after their initial impact, were no longer outrageous. On the contrary, they were now generally described as 'lovable' and the awarding of MBEs to all the group in 1963 was the ultimate symbol of acceptance by the establishment. Whilst this may well have been no more than a cynical move by the Wilson government to attract the youth vote, this endorsement of the swinging sixties was indicative of the taming process which would result in the commercialisation of Carnaby Street and the Kings Road and the triumph of style over substance in everything from fashion to fine art.

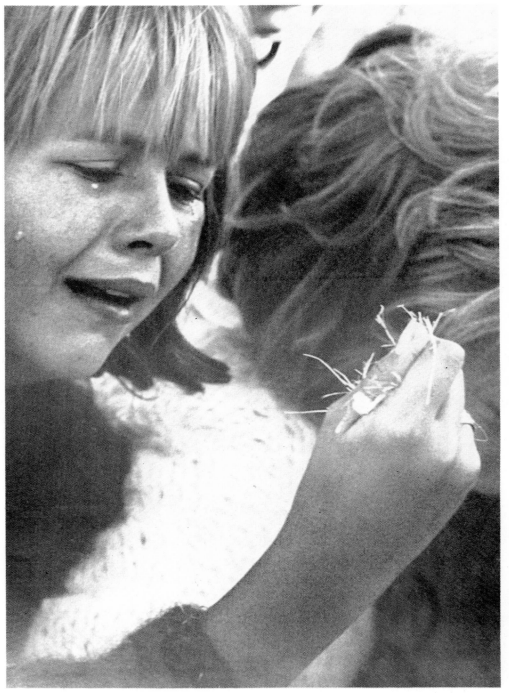

Left *Overcome by emotion, a fan clutches a tuft of grass trodden on by the Beatles during their first American tour.*

Right *America retained pre-eminence in pop as Art, exemplified by Roy Lichtenstein's comic strip images.*

The Rolling Stones' musical background was different from the Beatles', for their roots were in the blues and rhythm and blues, a minority musical taste in Britain where it was more closely associated with jazz than pop. Unlike the Beatles, they were not professionals (Mick Jagger was a student at the London School of Economics and only quit in 1963 when the Stones' success was assured), nor did their manager, Andrew Oldham, unlike Epstein, seek to make them acceptable. What they did was to capitalize on the transitory shock qualities of the Beatles, guaranteeing that they would not share the same fate. In contrast to the Beatles' pretty love songs, the Stones' raw music allowed its black R & B roots to surface with sexual energy, whilst visually they eschewed stage suits and neat hair. As the Beatles' appeal was more widely marketed and their fans got younger (leading to the teeny-bopper phenomenon), so the Stones and those whose sucess sprang from them – the Animals and the Pretty Things, for example – remained a vibrant force. Around them the era's ideal of meritocracy began to slide towards mediocrity, as 'trendiness' became the yardstick by which design, the arts and even politics were judged.

Below *Following the Beatles' success the arrival of the Rolling Stones in the USA established the pre-eminence of British pop.*

Right *Psychedelic posters, originally street art, became the acid heraldry of flower power.*

The Stones Blast Through the Land

clean, simple lines and who, to an extent, adapted other designers' work, most particularly Courregès's mini skirt, which she popularised to the extent that it became synonymous with 'swinging Britain'. Biba promoted the kitsch look. In terms of fashion, kitsch continued the eclectic style of the Individualists who had been eclipsed by the Mod movement. More widely, the playfulness and eccentricity the style embodied helped to create the dominant British image of the decade. Nostalgia was a major constituent of this post-war kitsch, which had its roots in the Black Eyes and Lemonade exhibition (Whitechapel Art Gallery 1951) and the Victorian element in the Festival of Britain. The consequence was contrary movements in design and feeling so that, at the same time that Harold Wilson was painting the image of a new Britain 'forged in the white heat of [this] scientific revolution' (1963), there was a mood of nostalgic affection for many elements of a vanishing age, as indicated by the fact that *Steptoe and Son* became the most popular television show of the time. Thus although British Railways, in the spirit of the time, shortened its name to British Rail and embarked upon a comprehensive programme of modernizing its image, involving the design of new logo and livery and the restyling of everything from staff uniform to buffet cutlery, there was also nostalgia for the pre-Beeching Victorian station. Incidentally the updating of names became a sixties fetish. The destruction of the traditional Lyons Corner House tea-rooms, which had begun in the fifties, culminated in a belated revival under the trendy abbreviation of 'Jolyon'. Similarly, the modernisation of the traditional pub, which resulted in the destruction by the breweries of many Victorian landmarks, spawned an interest in Victoriana. The anniversary of

Left *By 1969 the mini had become just another style.*
Right *Yves Saint Laurent's 1966 trouser suit in rich velvet with satin embellishments.*

the beginning of the 1914-18 World War, which received extensive press coverage, also contributed to visual nostalgia, which was to become incorporated into Carnaby Street pop through the I was Lord Kitchener's Valet boutique. In particular, the transfer-decorated coffee mug which became a virtual epidemic at the time has its origins in Victorian and early 20th century commemorative china.

The Union Jack became a popular decorative motif, and its iconocalistic display on a variety of Carnaby Street products was seen as indicative of the anti-etablishment mood of the time. As a symbol of Britain's imperial past, it occupied an ambivalent position in the Sixties, its adoption by Carnaby Street spread into a general kitsch usage, such as Oliver Goldsmith's 1966 Union Jack sunglasses, and the Who, embodying the pop-art oriented Mod look, featured it in their clothes. Paradoxically, it almost simultaneously reverted to its original role during the temporary revival of patriotism surrounding Britain's triumph in the 1966 World Cup, as well as being used by manufacturers capitalising on the popularity of all things British. The 'I'm Backing Britain' campaign of 1968 naturally used it as their logo, advocating that it should be shown on all British goods. However at the same time the re-emergence of Mosley-style racialism, this time directed against the immigrant communities by the National Front, brought the emblem into disrepute with its 'British Bulldog' connotations. This 'pop' use of the Union Jack occured alongside an interest in old enamel advertising signs, Victorian toys, tins and packaging, fun fair art and seaside imagery, all of which showed a whimsical rejection of the new Britain of high-rise flats and concrete.

Below '*We Live Pop Art*' *claimed the Who in 1965, as can be seen in Pete Townsend's Union Jack jacket and Keith Moon's target motif sweater.*

Right *A bowler hat and the Union Jack symbolize Britain in this 1969 American advertisement.*

Although new forms of stylistic nostalgia would surface later in the decade, such as the influence on graphics of the works of Arthur Rackham and Aubrey Beardsley and of art nouveau and art deco, by 1966 it was firmly established as a counterbalance to Modernism. Social nostalgia was evoked in the Beatles' requiem for the traditional urban community in 'Penny Lane', and matched by the success of ITV's *Coronation Street*. Similarly, the 1966 movie *Blow-Up* (seen at the time as an only slightly romanticized picture of the cult of the folk-hero fashion photographer) included a sequence in which the hero purchases a World War I aeroplane propeller as a decor item, whilst on television John Steed's vintage Bentley in *The Avengers* marked him as a new, trendy Establishment figure. The image of even Whitehall having a hidden streak of romance, danger and eccentricity was also promoted in the emerging James Bond cult; the films *Dr No* (1963), *Goldfinger* (1964) and *Thunderball* (1965) progressively took Bond from Fleming's original concept into fantasies of high-tech gimmickry, sex, and, through Sean Connery, an element of self parody. A more realistic-seeming spy also came to the screen in *The Spy who came in from the Cold* (1965).

007 AFTER SHAVE

"When you use 007 ...be kind"

Cologne, After Shave, Deodorants, and other grooming aids. © 1967, Colgate-Palmolive Company

Far left *Sean Connery in* Goldfinger, *1964.*

Left *The James Bond cult was further exploited as a popular marketing image.*

Spying was a topical subject — the case of Gordon Lonsdale, Peter and Helen Kroger (1961), George Blake, the same year, William Vassall (1962), Greville Wynne (1962), Kim Philby (1969) and the Christine Keeler scandal (1963) all publicising the cloak-and-dagger aspects of the cold war. Espionage had become so fashionable that the spy camera, the Minnox, enjoyed a following for its chic high-tech.

British cinema was also enjoying a boom. In 1960 the only British film to receive international recognition was *Saturday Night and Sunday Morning*, a film in the social-realist tradition which was maintained in *A Taste of Honey* (1962), *The L-Shaped Room* and *This Sporting Life* (both 1963). This pattern of bleakness was broken in 1963 by the success of *Tom Jones*, which received Academy Awards for best film and best director, and the first Bond film, *Dr No*. In 1974 'British' films — not necessarily British made but dominated by British presence — triumphed. *Goldfinger* out-grossed everything, making Sean Connery a top star — no mean achievement in the year which saw *My Fair Lady* win eight Oscars, as well as the arrival of *Mary Poppins*. Peter Sellars starred in *Dr Strangelove* and *The Pink Panther*, directed by Blake Edwards. *Cinema Noir* was represented by *Becket*, *The Pumpkin Eater* and *The Servant*. Despite these achievements, the film most expressing the spirit of the time was the Beatles' *A Hard Day's Night*. Although directed by an American, Dick Lester, who a year later further demonstrated his affinity with the British scene in *The Knack*, the film capitalized on the granular black and white of *cinema verité* that had characterised the quality British sixties films, at the same time adding an almost surreal pace through fast cutting. This was the first pop film to have been distinctive in style.

Left The Avengers: *Diana Rigg and Patrick McNee*
Right *In 1963 Christine Keeler became notorious in the Profumo scandal.*

Although the next Beatles film *Help* (1965) continued the same humorous theme, its use of colour, exotic location and cameo studies of the individuals revealed the influence of the wider market of Beatlemania, particularly the USA. *Help* became the blueprint on which the synthetic American Beatle-clones, the Monkees, were modelled. Meanwhile, not only did the success of *A Hard Day's Night* inspire a host of British pop movies – *Ferry 'cross the Mersey* (Gerry and the Pacemakers, 1965), *Catch Us If You Can* (Dave Clark Five, 1964), *Saturday Night Out* (The Searchers, 1964), *Work is a Four Letter Word* (Cilla Black, 1965), it also opened the door to the Swinging Sixties movies, *Casino Royale* and *The Magic Christian*.

The term 'swinging Britain' had been publicized by the American *Time* magazine in its 1965 report on this apparent overnight transformation but 'swinging' was already in general usage alongside Beatnik slang, such as 'fab', 'rave' and 'gear', which had come into common use via the Beatles. It had been a jazz term since the forties but it was probably popularized on television by presenter, Norman Vaughan, who, with thumbs up, made it a catchphrase for approval, as oposed to 'dodgy' (thumbs down) for disapproval. Now that it was branded with the trendy epithet 'swinging' and coupled with the blatantly commercial interests that lay behind style, the protest against convention which had fuelled the early

sixties transformation became self-conscious and lost its subversive power. In many ways, only the face of the Establishment had changed. For the rest of the decade, the perspectives changed as real radicalism took to the streets, whilst chic radicalism (in the person of John Lennon) took to its bed.

Opposite *Women's Liberation became a political and social issue. In 1969 the American group N.O.W. urged secretaries to 'stop licking stamps and boots'.*

Below *Dave Clark in* Catch Us If You Can.

LIFE

FAYE DUNAWAY IN A '30s REVIVAL

BONNIE
Fashion's New Darling

JANUARY 12 · 1968

35¢

CHAPTER TWO

FLOWER POWER

Protest dominated the 1960s. Inocuous though they may now seem, the Beatles, the Rolling Stones, Bob Dylan, Andy Warhol, Mary Quant, Vidal Sassoon, John Stephens – virtually any major pop figure from that age – was heralded, at least in their early days, as 'revolutionary'. Throughout the decade, anti-Establishment figures, including such a motley collection as Bonnie and Clyde, Butch Cassidy, Ho Chi Minh, Mao and Che Guevara, became folk heroes. Although such minor manifestations of cultural trends can appear insignificant, taken together they are symptomatic of the underlying disaffection of a decade where many latent social and political issues were brought into the open – women's rights, sexual emancipation, Black civil rights, the role of workers and students, consumers' rights.

One of the decade's best-known and gentlest forms of protest came from the Flower Power movement. Despite its cosmic consciousness, the early days of the phenomenon were very much a re-affirmation of the Americanism which had been steadily eroded since the late fifties. American youth had enjoyed a temporary injection of identity with the surfacing and hot rod culture of the Beach Boys and Jan and Dean but, since then, the British invasion of the Beatles, the Rolling Stones and, of all things, Herman's Hermits, as well as British film and fashions, had taken away the international dominance of American popular culture that had characterized the fifties. The rejection of a materialistic society dominated by large corporations and high-pressure marketing had its roots in the previous decade, which was already showing signs of revolt against conspicuous con-sumerism. Nor should the adoption of a drug culture come as a surprise to parents who, during the flower children's formative years, had themselves been a nation of tranquillizer users, as well as consumers of vast quantities of patent medicines and slimming pills.

Opposite Bonnie and Clyde *(1968) inspired a cult retro fashion.*

Below *1969: the Women's Liberation Movement began public demonstrations.*

Above *Psychedelia spread from its origins in the San Francisco music poster and became a major graphic style in 1967.*

The search for personal identity also had a precedent in the boom in psychiatry which had occurred in the fifties. There was a precedent too for the search for the real America, though this was now a matter of hitch-hiking (or psychedelic VW buses, scaled down versions of Kensey's magic bus) rather than piling into the brand new duo-tone-plus-features family car that had filled the highways of the fifties, as the ad man's ideal suburban family travelled a country that was increasingly looking the same (courtesy of Howard Johnson, McDonalds and Texaco). It is ironic that, of fifties road literature, it would be Kerouac rather than General Motor's copyrighters whose latent images won the minds of the sixties.

The aesthetics of Flower Power look like a theme park composite of America's folk history. Navajo jewelry, beads and blankets hark back to the 19th century romantic image of the 'noble savage', further endorsed in the mescaline cult book *Don Juan, the Teaching of a Yacqui Indian*. Further images of the American Indian (owing more to fifties cowboys film than any real understanding) also appeared in the choice of tepees as the symbolic and occasionally actual ideal home for ex-urban commune dwellers. Commune living, with the ideal of the tribe as portrayed in *Hair*, also derived inspiration from the 17th century English Diggers and the 19th century American Oneida community, though actual existing examples of American anti-materialist, ideological societies, the Shakers, the Hutterites and the Amish were not followed, being, no doubt, too purist to serve as role models. The ideals of the tribe or family, in the sense of the extended family (which was itself to serve as a microcosm of the global family), stemmed from the quest for an alternative social structure. The desire for a fresh start (which, in extreme form, saw the taking of new, usually fanciful names in the same way that the Black Power disciples would renounce their 'slave' names) was mirrored in the film

Surrounded by posters with Indian motifs, Julie Christie models a hippie Indian leather breechclout and beads.

Planet of the Apes and renewed interest in the 1950 novel *The Earth Abides*, both of which explored the theme of a world purged by nuclear war. These experiments in communal family or tribal life took countless forms, from the faded 19th century houses, long since reduced to slum apartments, which were the spiritual home of flower power, to rural retreats. The famous Drop City in Colorado was distinguished by its home-built village of geodesic domes made from a variety of materials, including panels from wrecked autos, but couldn't survive the unequal struggle between idealistic intentions and the harsh reality of economics. Others, like the ill-fated Hog Farm, foundered as drug abuse, unsanitary living conditions, malnutrition and even violence sapped the spirit of the Love Generation. At its worst, the idea of the group manifested itself in the extreme religious fanaticism of Jim Jones' People's Temple or the satanic Manson 'family'.

Above *Red Indian crafts and imagery were popularized by the hippie movement.*

The commercialisation of the psychedelic poster was echoed in the insidious rise of the self-contradictory hippie industry. Head shops, which had been selling pipes and such esoteric items as (sometimes beautifully crafted) roach holders, as well as the work of local jewellers, leather and bead workers, began to find a tourist trade advertising the city as if it were Disneyland. It was romanticized in a series of songs: the Flowerpot Men's 'Let's Go to San Francisco', Scott MacKenzie's 'If You're Going to San Francisco (be sure to wear a flower in your hair)', and Eric Burdo's 'San Francisco Nights'. The latter was especially spurious, referring to the nights as warm, whereas, in fact, the chill Bay Area wind ensured that they were generally not. The city's climate threw many newcomers, whose impressions of California had been formed through the non-stop summer surfing songs of the Beach Boys, and who came dressed for 'warm San Francisco nights'. The combination of being underdressed, together with the effects of drug consumption, resulted in shivering hippies being a more common sight than the idealised beautiful people of Flower Power mythology.

Left *A General Electric ad from 1968 demonstrates how the images of Flower Power were soon exploited.*

Right *The singer Cher, then partnered by former husband Sonny, was a leading exponent of early Flower Power style in 1965.*

Above *The short-lived topless look was thinly veiled in Rudi Gernreich's 1964 see-through blouse.*

The reality was rather less utopian. Most of the city remained unaffected, with its traditional jangling cable cars and Fisherman's Wharf, the grim spectre of Alcatraz and, across the bay the pretty artists' colony of Sausalito, still attracting tourists. There was now, though, a new sleazier image, for the removal of inhibitions, the sexual revolution that characterized the age, had produced an explosion of commercialized sex. The topless craze originated as a serious statement by the feminist movement and was subsequently adopted by high fashion; in 1964 Gerreich sold some 3,000 topless swimsuits, while Yves St Laurent introduced a look which was essentially topless, save some diaphanous chiffon. On a seedier level, however, the fashion was taken up by the 'go-go' dancers who entertained in the new topless bars. Some establishments had topless go-go girls dancing in booths or cages outside, with one such contraption mounted on a pylon, spot-lit at night. The craze spawned even more bizarre variations. There were restaurants with topless waitresses, topless shoe-shine parlours, the Topless Mother of Eight and the Topless Grandma.

The hippies mainly confined themselves to Candlestick Park and the Haight-Ashbury district, although they could also be found panhandling in Union Square and outside fashionable restaurants. Their numbers swollen by a lemming-like influx which mirrored the 19th century California gold rush, the hippie movement had lost much of its initial innocence and idealism. The music was, by now, in the hands of major record companies and organised crime had moved into the drug scene.

Right *The topless swimsuit (1964) created a sensation, provoking complaints from scandalized critics.*

The 'crash pads' which filled the slum tenements were now filled to bursting and newcomers found that, instead of being welcomed in by the first generation, they were obliged to live on the streets. Believing in the 'warm San Francisco nights', their only protection, blankets and ponchos, were insufficient and soon simple exposure added new casualties to a growing sicklist of the victims of bad drugs and bad food. The movement was further weakened as it became fashionable. Weekend hippies avoided dropping out but could play at it with the psychedelic outfits now supplied by the fashion industry. There were hippie wings and even peel-off psychedelic stickers that enabled a car to make a transitory appearance as a 'love bug' with no lasting effect on its paintwork or trade-in value. The dressing-up aspect of pseudo-hippiedom was summed up in Barbie doll's 1967 Flower Power outfit. By now, sightseeing bus trips were taking in the Haight-Ashbury Freak show as part of their San Francisco itinerary, with camera-wielding tourists on the streets, mingling with international television crews and the increasing number of distraught parents searching for their truant children, many of whom were by now only too ready to drop back into the society they had rejected.

The demise of the San Francisco scene did not mean the end of the hippie era. Other cities were now playing host to the alternative society, which had also discovered that, though dispersed, it could unite in instant transient 'cities' – the festivals. Taking inspiration from the Newport Jazz Festival, these events (though soured by the violence of Altamont) have become an integral part of the music scene. The Monterey pop festival, 1967, (immortalised in the 1968 film *Monterey Pop*) established the reputations of Janis Joplin and Jimi Hendrix and ensured that appearances at subsequent major festivals, climaxing in Woodstock (July 1969) which had an attendance of some 450,000, would be almost mandatory for top performers.

Below *The ill-fated Janis Joplin emerged from Big Brother and the Holding Company to international fame after Monterey Pop.*

Right *Jimi Hendrix had formerly played with the Little Richard Band before becoming the ultimate acid rock guitar hero.*

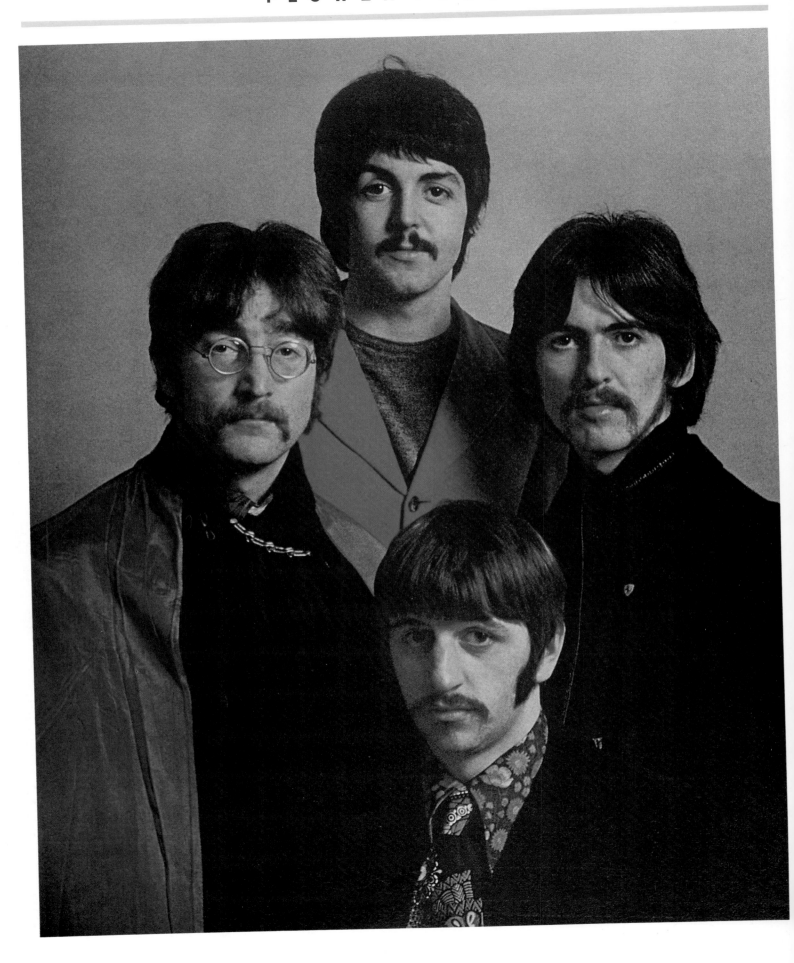

By 1968, the theatrical celebration of the Age of Aquarius in the form of the musical *Hair* was already overtaken by the harsher issues of Vietnam and civil rights, as well as by its own dark side revealed at Altamont and in the Manson case. Nevertheless, Flower Power had made its mark on the era. Although predominantly an American phenomenon, Europe too went through the experience – particularly England, which incorporated it into its own swinging image. The Beatles, pioneering the conceptual album with *Sergeant Pepper*, gave their seal of approval to the drug culture and became involved in Eastern mysticism. When Brian Epstein died in August 1967, two months after the release of *Sergeant Pepper*, it seemed a symbolic severance of the last links between the original Beatles

–clever, boisterous, innovative – and the new, introspective, other-worldly disciples of the Maharishi Mahesh Yogi. In reality, the Beatles had long since outgrown Epstein, but the apparent overnight conversion to meditation (they were on retreat with the Maharishi in Wales when Epstein died) coupled with the recent appearance of Yoko Ono on the scene, alienated many Beatle fans and broke the magic spell they had cast since the onset of Beatlemania. As a purely studio band, however, they had no affinity with the San Francisco psychedelic groups, whose extended solos and indulgent stage acts (The Grateful Dead were particularly known for disjointed, stoned performances during which a song could carry on until ennui set in) proclaimed a new, non-commercial approach.

Left *The Beatles (pictured in 1967) had taken popular music and culture into a new dimension of experimentation and mysticism.*

Below *George Harrison's interest in the sitar brought the virtuoso Ravi Shankar an international audience.*

Although it had been the American band, Jefferson Airplane who had drawn an acid analogy with Lewis Carrol in their psychedelic anthem 'White Rabbit', English Psychedelia placed even greater emphasis on a heritage of literture and art for which it felt an affinity. There was renewed interest in Tolkien, De Quincy, William Blake and Richard Dadd, and they shared with the pre-Raphaelites, whose images seemed close to the English romantic flower power look, a fascination with Merlin and the Arthurian legends. Some, seeking ancient wisdoms, became followers of Druidism.

Much of this served to emphasize the purity of the psychedelic movement in contrast to the commercial pop scene, so that by the time the Rolling Stones gave a free concert in Hyde Park in 1969 there appeared nothing incongruous in Mick Jagger, wearing a white dress, reading lines from Shelley's *Adonais* as a eulogy for Brian Jones, who had died three days before.

Above *The vastness of open-air festivals seemed to confirm the optimistic feeling of universal harmony.*

Right *White butterflies were released over the audience for the Rolling Stones' Hyde Park concert which had unexpectedly become a memorial to Brian Jones.*

Nevertheless, there was a growing rift between the grass roots underground movement, who, like their American contemporaries were developing an alternative culture through music, arts labs and their own press, and the new establishment as exemplified by Apple. The Apple Boutique, during its brief existence, had little to distinguish it from other psychedelic emporia such as Granny Takes a Trip and Hung On You, and other Apple activities also seemed indicative of the declining positon of the Beatles as role models. Although commercially successful (six weeks at number one in the 1968 charts, surpassing the Beatles' own 'Lady Madonna' and 'Hey Jude'), Apple's 'Those Were the Days', sung by their new protegée, Mary Hopkin, was insipid and folksy in the Eurovision Song Contest tradition. Although of that year's chart hits only Arthur Brown's 'Fire' had the sound of the British underground, it was nevertheless a reflection on the Beatles' remoteness from the scene that they could be involved in such blandness. Even more indicative was that, in pursuit of enlightened capitalism it seemed that, at least for a while, they genuinely believed that through their patronage they could bring about technological breakthroughs which were eluding the conventional research of universities and industry. Much of this was to be achieved through their electronics division, which was in reality a young inventor called Magic Alex. Unfortunately, one of their projects was the development of a device to stem the loss of royalties resulting from unauthorized taping of records. The Capitalist Society is dead – long live Capitalism.

As it turned out, the Beatles soon became disenchanted with what Lennon described as 'Apple and all this junk and The Fool and all the stupid clothes and all that'. Furthermore, playing at being businessmen was proving financially disastrous: 'People were robbing us and living on us out of Apple and nobody was doing anything about it.

All our buddies that worked for us for fifty years were all just living and drinking and eating like fuckin' Rome . . . ' (Lennon). Although the music side of the business was more complex to unravel, the Apple boutique was closed with a stylish finale. In the manner of the sardonic humour of *The Magic Christian* (whose wealthy, cynical hero once opened a shop where goods were surrealistically cheap in order to watch human greed at work), the Beatles ceased to be retail entrepreneurs by simply giving the stock away.

Above *Peter Sellars and Ringo Starr in* The Magic Christian, *a bizarre satire on human greed.*

Below *Heavily stylized psychedelic typography became a cliché in advertisements aimed at the youth market.*

General Motors Delco Car Stereo.

Take it out on a drab day. A rainy day. Right into a sullen traffic jam. Then turn it on.

Suddenly, your world is sunshine! Roses! Bright colors! A world on wheels you never thought possible! You see, Delco stereo systems are made especially for GM cars. The front-rear speakers are acoustically tailored to each body style to fill your car with a sound that's fantastically rich and real. A sound you can get two ways:

First, with Delco AM/FM Stereo Radio for varied programming.

Or go with the 8-track StereoTape system. Then you can pick a number, any number. And take it with you anywhere.

But you've really got to hear it for yourself. Test drive a Delco Stereo in a new Chevrolet, Pontiac, Oldsmobile, Buick or Cadillac. Ask for one with Delco FM Stereo. Or Delco StereoTape. Or both.

And let the rest of the world dull by.

Delco Radio, Division of General Motors.

The Apple Boutique was an anachronism, owing more to the Carnaby Street of Swinging London than the alternative society, and its demise belatedly closed that era. Not only had London been temporarily eclipsed by San Francisco, but the global village had, in a way, become a reality. The hippie movement had done much to erode national identities. For the first time under peace conditions, large numbers of young people were travelling (though this trend was soon to be augmented by Vietnam draft dodgers fleeing to Canada and Europe). India and North Africa were favourites for exotic travel, whilst Amsterdam beckoned as the drug centre of Europe.

The Amsterdam hippies were unique in bringing a political sense to the movement, anticipating Jerry Rubin's 'yippies' in the USA. In an attempt to solve city traffic problems, the hippies introduced the white bicycle scheme. The rationale of this was that 'public property' bicycles, distinguished by being painted white, should be for free use. One could simply take one from the street, abandoning it at the end of the journey where it could be found for its next user.

Though something of a new development among hippies, this kind of specific social protest became more prominent towards the end of the sixties, supplanting the undirected quest for an alternative society. The protests were fuelled by the Establishment's response to certain aspects of that quest, for one major result of the drug culture had been the socially divisive effects of anti-drug legislation and its enforcement. Quite simply, more people from all walks of life were being busted: one of the most enduring visual images of the period is Richard Hamilton's 'Swinging London 1967' series, utilizing a press picture of Mick Jagger handcuffed to the art gallery owner, Robert Fraser, after being arrested on a drugs charge. The widespread disrespect for the Law and Authority encouraged by anti-drug activities helped to creat a climate in which political

Stoned kids think they can handle it

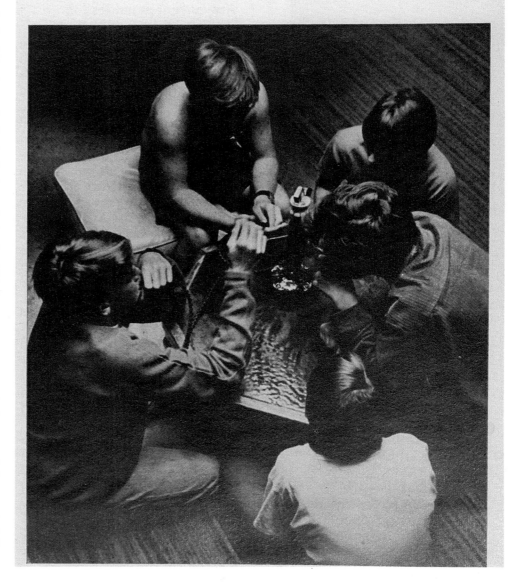

confrontation became a natural development. This was particularly traumatic in Britain, whose class system had ensured that most of society had little contact with law enforcement, which had enjoyed an uncritically high reputation.

Opposite *Jerry Rubin emerged in 1968 as spokesman for the 'Yippies' – politically aware hippies.*

Above *The drug culture became almost synonymous with the alternative society, and, for the press, the most newsworthy aspect of it.*

Paradoxically, whilst the British legal system came under increasing attack, there occurred several legislative landmarks towards liberalization. The Sexual Offences Act, 1967, de-criminalized homosexual acts, save in a few circumstances; the same year also saw the general legalization of abortion. The following year restrictions on divorce were reduced (and further legislation in 1969 made the breakdown of a marriage the only criterion for divorce), and the Lord Chamberlain's office lost the power, which it had exercised since the 17th century, to censor theatrical productions. To celebrate this event, *Hair* opened in London the next day, its fleeting moment of stage nudity heralded as a major landmark in artistic freedom, though it was later, with Kenneth Tynan's *Oh Calcutta!* in 1970, that stage nudity became more than a token gesture, for *Hair* coyly dimmed its stage lights almost immediately its cast revealed themselves. 1968 also saw the Race Relations Act, which made racial discrimination a criminal offence. The only overtly oppressive legislation of this time was the Marine Broadcastig Act, which closed down most of the pirate radio stations.

Nevertheless, the image of a repressive Establishment persisted, and the dominant theme of the late sixties in Britain, as well as in Europe and the USA, was of protest and confrontation.

Top right *The stage musical* Hair, *celebrating the 'Age of Aquarius', lost its shock value by becoming a box-office hit.*

Bottom right *The commune dwellers of Drop City constructed scrap metal geodesic housing.*

Left *The beat poet Allen Ginsberg took to the streets in 1968 to champion the legalization of pot.*

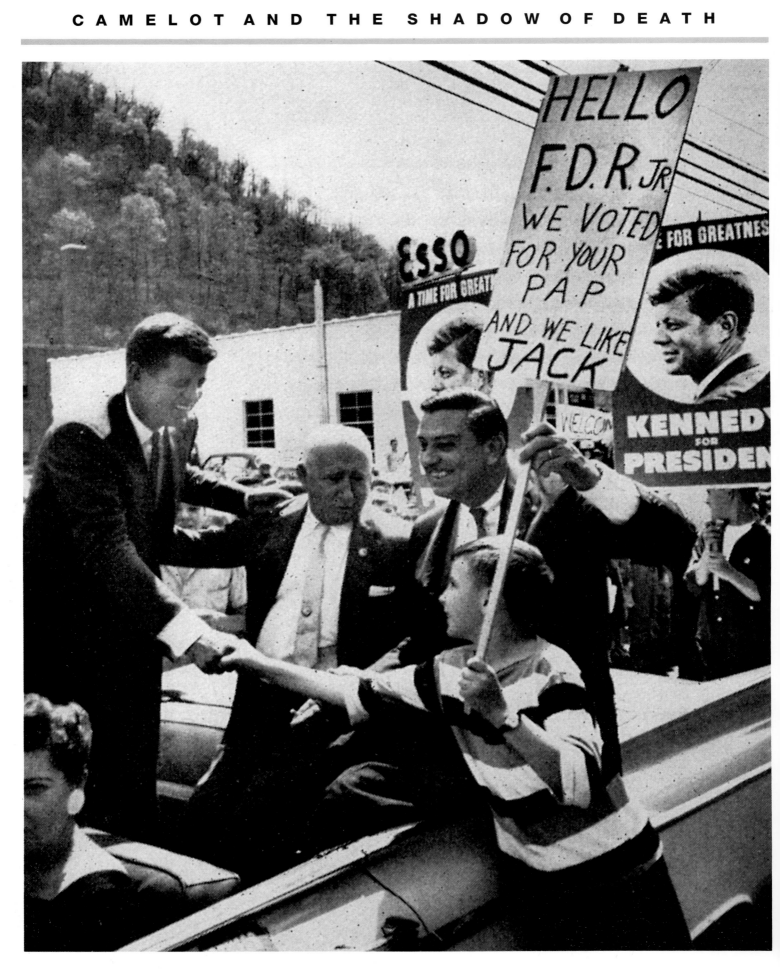

CHAPTER THREE

CAMELOT AND THE SHADOW OF DEATH

*'It may be he shall take my hand
And lead me into his dark land
And close my eyes and quench my breath
But I've a rendezvous with death.'*

John F. Kennedy claimed that this poem, *I Have a Rendezvous with Death* by Alan Seeger, was his favourite — a morbid choice, it would seem, for a young man who, fate would decree, did not outlive his image of youthful optimism. Yet death impinged on his early manhood. In active service in the US Navy in the war he was rescued from a sea covered in burning fuel after Japanese action sank his boat. A year later his brother Joe was killed in action; so, a month later, was his brother-in-law. He himself believed that he had a form of leukaemia and would not live past his forty-fifth year.

To the world, however, Kennedy, his wife and children epitomized beauty, youth, wealth and culture. In thousands of photographs of this young family relaxing they are so close to the model family of advertising myth that it only needs a prominently-shown station wagon, soft drink, soap or toothpaste to complete the picture. They seemed to embody the American ideal so exactly that it seems incredible that Kennedy's politics could not have been sold to the electorate as easily as a can of cola. With crusading political ideals to complement his immaculate image, Kennedy seemed perfect for the new decade — so much so that it must be remembered that he was not, in fact, an overwhelmingly popular choice, gaining the presidency over Nixon by only 120,000 votes.

The United States were ripe for social reform: the prosperity the country had enjoyed during the fifties had left behind a sufficiently large number of people for poverty to be a major problem, and civil rights issues — especially racial ones — were increasingly prominent in the public consciousness.

Opposite *Franklin Roosevelt Junior joined Kennedy in an electioneering rally, 1960.*

Below *The Kennedy clan's children, shown with Robert Kennedy in 1968.*

Moreover, national self-confidence had been undermined. By the end of the fifties the doctrine of conspicuous consumption which had been central to the American domestic economy had been discredited. The artificial stimulus of planned obsolescence had logically led to a reduction in the quality of goods, with a demoralizing effect on the consumer, who was beginning to revolt against the intensive marketing and social pressure of the Acquisitive Society. This revolt was supported by books and press articles questioning the morality of industry as well as the quality of its products. In many ways, the American Dream was becoming a nightmare; contemporary commentators cited the growing consumption of tranquillizers as evidence that society was becoming neurotic.

A further threat to the economy came from abroad. During the fifties Europe had rebuilt industries decimated by war and, although the American consumer society had become the model for the Western world, relative poverty had meant that Europe never experienced the extremes of planned obsolescence. The rejection of the spurious foundation of the American economy coincided with the arrival of European consumer products, with not only domestic appliances but more significantly, the very symbol of Americanism, the automobile, being challenged by imports.

Internationally, America was still locked in the cold war that had overshadowed the late fifties. The apparent thawing in the light of the fragile rapport established with Nikita Khrushchev disappeared with the shooting down in 1960 in Soviet airspace of an American U-2 plane, which Khrushchev alleged was on a spying mission. Although the West was unaware of it at the time, Soviet domestic politics were pressuring Khrushchev to backtrack on reconcilliation, with the result that he had used the U-2 incident of twelve days before to sabotage the Paris Peace Summit. Although the representatives of the other three powers – Eisenhower, MacMillan and de Gaulle – could not have prevented this debacle they were denied the result that, politically, their status as elder statesmen demanded. There was a feeling that the old generation had failed.

Above *De Gaulle's visit to Russia in 1966 was part of the mutual East-West effort to end the Cold War.*

Right *Leaders of conflicting cultures, Khruschev and Kennedy, in 1964.*

Below *Kennedy brought an almost evangelical atmosphere to politics with his idealism and conviction.*

Right *Bob Dylan brought the protest folk music from Greenwich Village coffee bars to an international audience.*

Kennedy was the new man; he promised change. His New Frontier campaign platform was a social regeneration programme with the same crusading image as Roosevelt's New Deal. Nixon, Kennedy's rival in the presidential race, warned that the cost of the reforms would impose a crippling tax burden, but the result, albeit close, affirmed Kennedy's repudiation of such materialism. His youthful vigour gave visual emphasis to his fresh idealism and to the contrast between himself, at 43 the youngest ever president, and Eisenhower, the oldest.

His inaugural address was pure evangelism. In a speech lasting only ten minutes he sounded ' the trumpet summons . . . against the common enemies or man: tyranny, poverty, disease and war itself.' He proclaimed a new era — 'The torch has been passed to a new generation of Americans' — and followed it with the memorable appeal to

the nation to reverse the materialism of the fifties: 'Ask not what your country can do for you — ask what you can do for your country.'

One thing Americans could do from 1961 was join the new Peace Corps and help — in the spirit of moral regeneration — not just their country but 'the great common cause of world development'. Volunteers were to live in Third World communities, giving practical assistance through teaching, medicine, building irrigation schemes and other projects. The appeal to idealism was in part a response to a domestic social problem. Although the protest movement was to be more a feature of the latter part of the decade, there was already evidence tht the young were disenchanted with society (in 1960 students demonstrating outside the House Committee on un-American Activities meeting in San Francisco had been doused with fire hoses and

beaten), and in seeking to channel youthful energy into the Peace Corps Kennedy was no doubt recognizing that in every level of society idealism would have to be put into positive and tangible action.

Altruistic though the Peace Corps may have been, there were suspicions that it served another purpose, as a pre-emptive strike against communism; there were rumours of CIA involvement. Despite his declared aim of world peace, Kennedy was well aware that the ideologies of East and West were still fighting for world supremacy. He had satisfied some of the doubters in his inaugural address by reassuring the nation that the quest for peace would not be at the expense of America's position in the world.

It was a similar need to boost morale at home, as well as to demonstrate America's technological superiority, that led to Kennedy's commitment to

YOUR MOST MEMORABLE EXPERIENCE
AT THE NEW YORK WORLD'S FAIR!
THE NEW **CINERAMA**®—360° PROCESS
TAKES **YOU...**

TO THE MOON AND BEYOND

BEYOND
BEYOND
BEYOND
BEYOND
BEYOND
BEYOND

the space programme, with the pledge that by the end of the decade they would put a man on the moon. Although the most obvious dividend of a successful space programme was prestige, there was another, hidden agenda. An advance in communications technology was to be the first tangible result — communications which could be put to use for propaganda, as well as military and commercial, purposes. By means of synchronized orbiting satellites, television programmes could be transmitted, via a ground station anywhere in the world. The influential science fiction writer, Arthur C. Clarke, who had foreseen satellites as long ago as the forties, had proposed in 1959 that communications were the key to winning the cold war, and that, by means of receivers not requiring ground stations, a superpower could subvert a country with television propaganda. Clarke claimed that the prize for being first with such a system could be 'whether fifty years from now, Russian or English is the main language of mankind'.

Above and **right** *Kennedy realized the propaganda value of space travel; to many it was the fulfilment of a science fiction fantasy.*

On April 12th 1961 Russia astounded the world by putting the first man, Major Yuri Gagarin, into space. The Vostok spacecraft made a single orbit of the earth at a height of 190 miles. Considering America's public commitment to bettering the Soviets, merely to duplicate this feat was insufficient. Hence the first American in space, US Commander Alan Shephard, despite only being in space for fifteen minutes, carried out manoeuvres, unlike Gagarin, who had been a mere passenger. On February 20th 1962, Lt. Colonel John Glenn became the first American to experience orbital flight by circling the planet three times. In the spirit of peace, the American craft was named Friendship 7. Three months later there was another, though less technically

successful, manned orbit. On both occasions the take-off and landing were shown live on television. In July 1962 an even more significant space event occurred with the launch of the first communications satellite, Telstar 1. The power of Telstar was dramatically proved when some 200 milion viewers in sixteen countries tuned in to watch television live from the USA.

Television, which had been a major political weapon since the early fifties, was now usurping the printed word as the main vehicle for news coverage. Kennedy made particularly strategic use of the medium during the Cuban Missile Crisis, publicly calling on Khrushchev to 'halt and eliminate this clandestine, reckless and provocative threat to world peace and to stable re-

lations between our two nations — to abandon this course of world domination and to join in an historic effort to end the perilous arms race and transform the history of man'. Whilst the world waited with bated breath, Soviet warships heading for Cuba turned back and negotiations for a settlement began. At home and abroad Kennedy's position as guardian of the West was now established. He had kept the promise made in his inaugural address.

Below *Telstar was the first application of space technology to have an impact on daily life.*

Right *Kennedy and Glenn in 1962 – euphoric in the realization of a dream.*

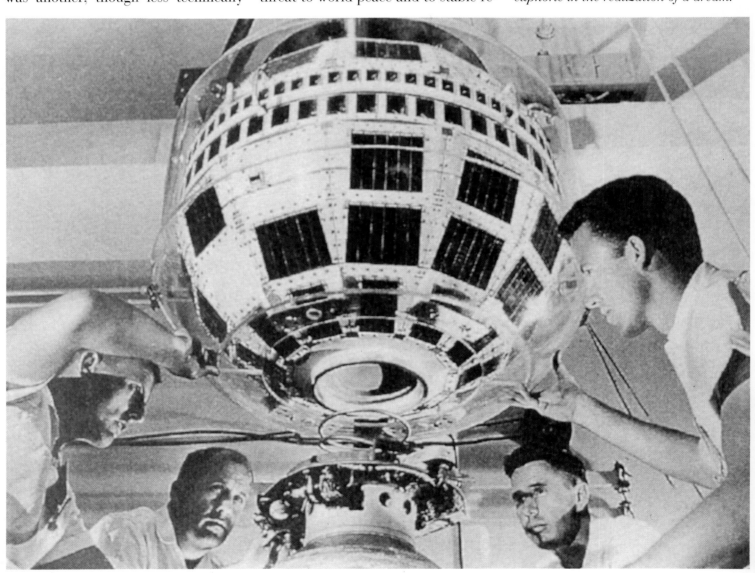

It was the same promise – to be aggressive in guarding America's interests throughout the world – that prepared the way for an event that was to cast a deep shadow over the rest of the decade. Little attention was given to an American announcement, in 1961, that it was to increase its token number of 700 'military advisers' to South Vietnam to 16,000, along with a full complement of hardware including aircraft, for which an airbase was being constructed. That year, James Davis became the first American serviceman to be killed by the Vietcong. The next year Kennedy also increased the American presence in Laos to strengthen America's commitment to countering the spread of communism in South East Asia. Under President Johnson the involvement escalated into war. Perhaps the real tragedy of America in the sixties was not so much the death of Kennedy but that the con-

By 1969 the realities of Vietnam had been revealed to a shocked world. **Left** *Combat.* **Above** *The black market thrived.*

flict in and over Vietnam would have the effect of counteracting, both morally and financially, the domestic regeneration he was promising.

From the beginning, though, his domestic policies, which were the heart of his election platform, proved difficult to implement. The greatest fear in the country had been neither the threat of the Soviets nor social and racial inequality, but the poor economy. Nixon's strongest counter-attack against the charisma of Kennedy was the high cost of the proposed social programme. Such ideals as a guaranteed minimum wage and medical care for the poor had limited appeal to a nation conditioned to consumerism. In terms of social equality the Kennedy years provided more questions than answers.

The myth that has grown since Kennedy's death may have simplified the public memory of the man and his popularity. His image was immaculate, but there remained enough opposition to his ideas, in Congress and on the street, to ensure that his brief stay in the White House, despite appeals to patriotism and ideology, was characterized as much by dissent as support. Even in the anguished aftermath of Dallas, when the world went into shock, there were those who saw the assassination as a salvation. CBS TV broadcast an account by a Dallas minister of comforting a fourth-grade class teacher traumatized by the joyful reaction of the children when she broke the news of the assassination – a sinister reflection of their parents' attitudes to Kennedy.

The antagonism between the apparently ideal Kennedy and the country he presided over was not solely due to his liberalism. Although he and his family may have had the look of the American Dream, there was much that was alien, to the point of being un-American. There was a strong European flavour to his political conduct – the influence of his short period as a student at the London School of Economics, as well as the extensive visits he made to England between 1937, when his father became American Ambassador to Britain, and 1941, when he

Below left *The harrowing photographs of Kennedy's assassination are still continually re-examined in the quest to discover new evidence.*

joined the US Navy. As a young man he had been impressed by Winston Churchill, and was to bring to his speeches a Churchillian sense of destiny which contrasted with rival Richard Nixon's professional pragmatism. Furthermore, his wife, Jacqueline, exuded European chic in her clothes, hairstyle and knowledge of French art and history. The image too readily brought to mind the growing influence of Europe on the American way of life.

On November 22 1963 Kennedy's assassination fulfilled his own morbid premonitions and when in the presence of the world's leaders the Last Post was sounded at his funeral, there could have been few not wondering whether the 'torch passed to a new generation' was now extinguished.

Above *Few people were unmoved by the tragic dignity of Kennedy's family at his state funeral.*

CHAPTER FOUR

THE BLACK MUSLIMS

*I*n 1960 the United States was facing two major social problems which the previous decade had begun to address: black civil rights and poverty which, although a black problem too, was nevertheless inter-racial.

Eisenhower's last few months in office were occupied with the build up of racial tension in the Southern States, centred on Montgomery, Alabama, where Martin Luther was urging government action to defuse the situation. The election of Kennedy intensified the issue. Alabama was the focal point for an increasingly assertive, though essentially peaceful, Black protest movement, which was fast gaining White liberal support. Within a few months of Kennedy's optimistic inaugural speech, Alabama Freedom Riders – black and white civil rights workers who had been flouting the State's segregationalist laws by riding public service buses – were physically attacked by mobs of segregationalists. As the protesters were already under a court injunction prohibiting 'riding', many were arrested for this breach, whilst the Reverend Martin Luther King, conducting a Church meeting on these events, had to be protected from another mob. In 1962 King was imprisoned for leading a civil rights march in Georgia and holding a public prayer meeting on church steps in protest against the persistent refusal of local politicians to honour their promises of talks.

Left *Vilified by both black activists and white segregationalists, Martin Luther King nevertheless brought Civil Rights to political prominence.*

Right *Ku-Klux Klan leader ('Imperial Wizard') Robert Shelton of Alabama poses before a blazing cross in 1965.*

Kennedy was obliged to intervene when the Governor of Mississippi, in defiance of a court order, blocked the admission of James Meredith, the first black student to enrol in the University of Mississippi. This blocking was quite literal: Meredith was barred by state troops acting on the Governor's orders. Dramatically Kennedy sent in 750 Federal Marshals, under the direct control of the Deputy Attorney-General, to protect Meredith and his suporters. The violent riots of the Meredith incident resulted in three deaths and fifty injuries. An escalation of violence now threatened the ideal of non-violent protest which had characterized the movement since the Freedom Riders began. King, like Gandhi in India, consistently emphasized the doctrine of non-violence: "We must have compassion and understanding for those who hate us. We must realise so many people are taught to hate us that they are not totally responsibly for their hate. But we stand in life at midnight, we are always on the threshold of a new dawn." For many, the patient working towards a 'new dawn' had been going on for too long.

Below *James Meredith pictured with his mother in 1966.*

Right *Comedian Dick Gregory specialized in using satire to attack segregation; here he spoofs the Klan in a 1961 sketch.*

To those who were becoming impatient with the martyrdom of nonviolence and those city dwellers who had little in common with the rural religious base of the Civil Rights Movement, the Black Muslims offered an alternative vision. The Black Muslim movement contrasted strongly with Martin Luther King's vision of peaceful integration. Their spokesman, Malcolm X, expressed their impatience with the slow progress of the Civil Rights Movement: "The black man in this country has been sitting on the hot stove for nearly four hundred years and no matter how fast the brainwavers and the brainwashed think they are helping him advance, it's still too slow for the man whose behind is burning on the hot stove." He was also dismissive of the popular comparison between King and Ghandi: "Ghandi was a big dark elephant sitting on a little white mouse. King is a little black mouse sitting on top of a big white elephant."

Although the Black Muslim Movement only began to make a wide impact following the demonstrations in Birmingham in 1963, it had been in existence since before 1930, its founder and leader, Elijah Muhammad, deriving his inspiration from the Arab Saviour, D W Ford. The differences between the Muslims and the Civil Rights Movement were fundamental, for the Muslims' goal was not equality: "The white devil's day is over. There is none a black man can trust. He was given six thousand years to rule, his time was up in 1914. These are his years of grace — seventy of them. He's already used up most of those years trapping and murdering the black nations by the hundreds of thousands. Now he's worried, worried about the black man getting his revenge."

Left *During this freedom march in 1965 a participant, Mrs Viola Liuzzo, was murdered. Four Klan members were charged.*

Below *Malcolm X converted to Islam whilst in prison for theft, eventually becoming leader of the Black Muslims.*

White liberals recoiled from the Muslims, hurt and bewildered by their uncompromising rejection. Not only did the Muslims reject integration, they also dismissed Christianity as a 'white' religion. Martin Luther King's Civil Rights Movement was based on the Southern Churches and drew its support from rural as well as urban communities, whereas the Muslims, with thirty mosques, mainly in the cities, including New York and Washington, drew members from a wider area. The Muslims demanded and enforced strict discipline from their members, including a ban on any activity that would confirm white stereotypes of black behaviour – music, singing, dancing, drinking and criminal activities. In Chicago the Muslims had their own, state-recognised school. The Muslims' declared aim was to make the United States a black nation and, in its pursuit, promoted a new black identity that was to become manifest in the ethos of Black Pride. Although the Muslims sought to avoid all contact with whites, including political confrontation, part of their training programme involved training in the martial arts, including a technique for fending off and then killing police dogs. Violence was now focusing attention on the Civil Rights Movement, which was receiving increased press and television coverage. The events in South Africa with the 1960 Sharpeville massacre and its tragic toll of fifty-six deaths and hundreds of casualties an ever-present

spectre, meant that violence – its use or avoidance – was a major issue. Pressmen covering the Movement were treated with suspicion by both segregationalists and civil rights activists. Photographer Charles Moore (whose photographs of the Martin Luther King-led Birmingham, Alabama demonstrations in 1963 were used in the congressional debate on the 1964 Civil Rights Act) stated, "I've been in Vietnam but I was never so frightened as I was in some places in the South . . .

With some white crowds you felt if they had guns they'd just as soon shoot you down." Nevertheless, reportage continued to keep the Movement in the public consciousness. Bill Reed's 1964 *Life* photograph of Sheriff Rainey and Deputy Price, with their supporters, mocking proceedings at their trial for the lynching of three Mississippi civil rights workers, was extensively reprinted in the national press, as well as appearing as a poster with the ironic caption 'Support your local police'.

Below *The Sharpeville massacre not only focused world attention on South Africa but also highlighted the danger civil rights workers faced in America.*

CONTINUED

Left *William Rogers (foreground), who had been paralyzed by police bullets, and Malcolm X display Black Muslim news sheets in 1963.*

Above *Champion boxer Cassius Clay converted to the Black Muslim faith, taking the name Muhammad Ali after initially calling himself Cassius X.*

As was later to be the case with Vietnam, television was the greatest factor in public awareness. Kennedy's election had symbolised the new mood of an America jaded with trivia and the dominance of commercial considerations. This had an effect on television, which began to screen hard-hitting documentaries, such as *Superfluous People* (WCBS-TV, Atlanta) on the subject of segregation.

Although King's eventual success in negotiating de-segregation with civic and business leaders in Birmingham seemed a vindication of his non-violent stance, he was facing increasing dissent from elements within the Movement who were advocating aggressive direct action. King now seemed to be addressing not only his immediate listeners but also the wider audience of press and television, allaying the fears that the Black Power Movement was beginning to engender with his moderating statements. In the wake of Birmingham he said, "We must not see the present victory as a victory for the negro. It is a victory for democracy . . . We must not be overbearing or haughty in spirit." To the younger, more militant black

leaders, including Malcolm X and Medgar Evans, King's approach was counter productive. 'Uncle Tomism' became the derisory term for simple de-segregation, in contrast to the emerging moves towards Black Consciousness and ultimately Black Power. The writings of Marcus Garvey became the inspiration for a total rejection of the 'Americanisation' which had swallowed black identity. Since slaves had been known by the surname of their master and their use was deemed to symbolically perpetuate slavery, Malcolm X and others renounced their 'slave names', the most famous such change being the champion boxer Cassius Clay's adoption of the name Muhammad Ali.

LIFE On the Newsfronts of the World

Freedom March Ends

Above *The violence which stalked freedom marchers proved counter-productive for the segregationalists, having the effect of increasing public sympathy for the Civil Rights Movement.*

King was in danger of becoming eclipsed by Malcolm X as the *de facto* black leader when violence resurfaced after Birmingham, culminating in the murder of Medgar Evans. The 1963 Civil Rights March was to become an historic landmark for the Movement. As well as being immortalized in the television documentary *The March*, massive news coverge brought King's "I have a dream" speech to millions of television viewers, in addition to his audience of some 200,000 marchers who had been joined by celebrities, including Marlon Brando, Burt Lancaster, Judy Garland and Bob Dylan and who were now gathered at Washington's Lincoln memorial. The attention given to the march resulted in a general liberalization of attitudes towards blacks, with corporations and television actively seeking to demonstrate their integrationist policies by putting them in positions of greater prominence, though often such gestures were no more than tokenism.

Nevertheless, within a month violence again erupted in the South. Governor George Wallace of Alabama ordered state troopers to prevent black pupils from entering a high school,

a Murder

which Kennedy countered by taking direct control of the Alabama National Guard to enforce the integration. In Birmingham, violence returned with four little girls killed and twenty-three people injured when a church service was bombed. A sixteen-year-old boy was fatally shot and many were injured in the subsequent rioting.

At this stage it appeared that, albeit reluctantly, public opinion was behind Kennedy on the civil rights issue. There was, however, the danger of a back-lash, with the most prominent pro-segregationalist, Governor George Wallace (who was elected in 1962 on an anti-civil rights ticket — "Segregation now, segregation tomorrow, segregation for ever") acting as unofficial spokesman for the diehards. As Kennedy's support in congress was only marginal Wallace presented a real threat. With the march on Washington making civil rights the main issue of the Kennedy era, Wallace took a confrontationalist stance. In June the University of Ala-

bama accepted two black students. Wallace banned their enrolment: "I am the embodiment of the sovereignity of this state and I will be present to bar the entrance of any negro who attempts to enrol at the University of Alabama." The news exposure the belligerent Wallace was getting made Alabama the High Noon of Kennedy's administration. Three thousand troops were sent into Alabama (an extraordinary number when set against the 5,000 sent to Vietnam the previous year) and Kennedy who, via his brother Robert, the US Attorney General, had been vainly trying to persuade Wallace to abandon his segregationalist stand (Robert commented "It's like a foreign country; there's no communication") decided that the whole confrontation should be documented on film. With the cameras ready, the stage was set for a confrontation of ideologies that had festered under the surface of America since the Civil War. The contrast between the protagonists — Wallace, a pugnacious boxing champion, now fighting for the old South, and the elegant privileged Kennedys, who not only hailed from the North East, land of the carpetbaggers, but what was worse were also Bostonians and Catholics — was the stuff of high drama. In the event, whilst Wallace literally guarded the University, the two students quietly entered the building by another route. The final film, containing behind the scenes action in the Kennedy camp and reportage on Wallace and his side, *Crisis, Behind a Presidential Commitment* was clearly a political move to force congressional support for Kennedy. The President declared "We face . . . a moral crisis as a country and a people. It cannot be met by repressive police action. It cannot be left to increased demonstrations in the streets. It cannot be quietened by token moves or talk. It is a time to act in Congress, in your state and local legislative body and, above all, in all of our daily lives." *Crisis, Behind a Presidential Commitment* was shown on television in October. A month later, Kennedy was dead.

Right *Martin
Luther King's 'I
have a dream'
speech became the
historic climax of
the pacifist Civil
Rights Movement.*

CHAPTER FIVE

DECADE OF PROTEST THE JOHNSON ERA

The historical tragedy of Dallas was not that the light of liberalism was extinguished – if anything, the Civil Rights Act of 1964 which, had Kennedy been alive, might not have got through Congress, became a posthumous tribute – but rather that the optimism went out of liberal politics. Lyndon Johnson, lacking the boyish charisma that had characterized Kennedy and had made his death so poignant, was doubly disadvantaged, stepping into a dead man's shoes without notice. His first public statement, directly televised in a sequence which only minutes before had shown Kennedy's coffin being lowered from Air Force One and the blood-stained Jacqueline Kennedy, was, of necessity, in stark contrast to the inaugural address with which Kennedy had heralded a new era. Johnson ended with the words: "I will do my best. That is all I can do. I ask your help – and God's!" The twin burdens that Johnson had inherited, the commitment to social justice and the Vietnam War, were both to result in his undeserved vilification as the decade of protest entered its most violent phase.

Whilst the civil rights issue dominated domestic policy, American involvement in Vietnam, almost unnoticed at home, was reaching a turning point. Even whilst Kennedy's body was still lying in state, Johnson was having to formulate a response to the murder, three weeks before Kennedy's, of South Vietnamese President Ngo Dinh Diem and his brother, who were overthrown by a military coup. Although the United States officially recognized the new South Vietnamese government and had had great reservations about the corrupt Diem regime, it now had to decide whether to increase US assistance. Failure to do so would probably mean the defeat of South Vietnam and a subsequent communist take-over of Indo-China, whose raw materials were deemed essential to the American economy.

Opposite *Lyndon and 'Lady Bird' Johnson.*

Above *The Kennedy torch passed to brother Robert, pictured here with Jackie in 1966.*

As 1964 was election year, Johnson kept his decision to increase American involvement in Vietnam a virtual secret until after the election and, although in August Congress gave approval for "all necessary action" to be taken against North Vietnam, no-one was aware of the future consequences of that decision. From 1964 the build up of American military forces accelerated: Johnson ordered retaliation following an abortive attack by North Vietnamese torpedo boats on a US destroyer. The next year saw rapid escalation, with US B52s carying out low-level attacks in North Vietnam and the first dramatic use of helicopter gunships. Marines were also sent to Vietnam to

Left *Carl Stokes became the first black to achieve high civic office when he was elected Mayor of Cleveland, Ohio in 1967.*

Above right *The writer James Baldwin (here photographed in 1963) drew attention to urban poverty.*

counter guerilla warfare. These were the first US troops specifically designated as fighters, the euphemistic term 'military advisers' now being obviously spurious. Despite American troops still being under the direction of South Vietnam, foreign criticism of US involvement began. World leaders, including the Pope and President de Gaulle, protested and, in what was to be a constant theme for the rest of the decade, there were violent demonstrations in front of the American Embassy in Paris.

To the American public, however, Johnson was the executor of Kennedy's civil rights policy, making television appearances to promote the proposed Civil Rights Law, even treating audiences to his singing of "We Shall Overcome!", anthem of the movement. With the increased press and television attention, the Civil Rights Movement began to gain wider liberal support, both with black and white, and volunteer 'Freedom Riders' went to the South to assist in community work. But opposition was equally intense.

In August 1964 the first major threat to the Kennedy/Johnson liberalism appeard when the Republican Convention nominated the right-wing Senator, Barry Goldwater, as its Presidential Candidate by a huge majority. Goldwater's main campaigning theme was the breakdown in law and order caused by liberal policies, and he embarked on a propaganda war, using television advertising in the documentary manner pioneered by Kennedy. Scenes from Black Civil Rights meetings were juxtaposed with images of rioting and of delinquent white juveniles; the rise in pornography and such manifestations as the topless fashion were shamelessly linked with civil rights issues. The theme was that East coast liberals were subverting the moral values of the nation. Sponsorship for these television broadcasts came from a wide range of supporters, including the Mothers for a Moral America. The John Birch Society, the prime anti-civil rights group, had also, by implication, received Goldwater's endorsement when his suporters blocked an attempt by Governor Rockefeller to have the Society censured at the Republican Convention. Goldwater's campaign also had the effect of focusing public attention on Vietnam, which both Kennedy and Johnson had contrived to keep almost secret. Right-wing military sources had told Goldwater that the war was going badly – information which he used as ammunition against Johnson. In the course of a television interview, Goldwater suggested a solution might be the use of a "low yield atomic device". This apparently casual attitude to atomic weapons, which received wide publicity, was the weapon Johnson needed to strike back, and he therefore used it to exploit the fears of atomic war which had been present through the fifties and right up to Cuba. Most famous of the television spots on this issue was the Daisy Girl – a short sequence showing a little girl picking petals off a daisy, to the background sound of a countdown, followed by an atomic explosion. As the screen went black, a voice said simply, "These are the stakes: to make a world in which all God's children live, or go into the dark."

Opposite *Senator Goldwater represented the reactionary challenge to liberalism at home as well as advocating aggression abroad.* **Above** *Topless fashion was pilloried as liberal decadence.*

The atomic threat was sufficient to counter Goldwater, whose campaign portrayed Johnson in a confusion of images as both liberal, in his role as Kennedy's heir, and, at the same time, as a Southern redneck. One notorious Goldwater propaganda film was a sequence of a speeding Lincoln from which beer cans were being thrown, a direct reference to a story that Johnson had been drinking whilst indulging in some fast driving near his Texas ranch. Meanwhile, the war in Vietnam was escalating. Johnson's triumph over Goldwater in the 1964 Presidential Election, polling sixty percent of the votes, was an endorsement of Kennedy's policies. This endorsement seemed confirmed by the fact that both Robert Kennedy who, as his brother's Attorney-General, had been responsible for

implementing civil rights and who was generally seen as the driving force behind Kennedy's confrontations with anti-segregationalists, and his other brother, Edward, now became senators. How much of the vote was due to outside forces cannot be determined but three international events which occurred the month before the election must be considered major factors.

The removal of Nikita Krushchev deprived the West of its link with Russia. Although Krushchev had fulfilled his bogeyman role with gusto, he had established a reputation as a personality that the West could, despite his unpredictability, relate to. Following the Cuban Crisis, a hotline had been set up between Moscow and Washington in 1963, thus recognising a shared dread of atomic confrontation. At the

same time, Russia had entered into a Nuclear Test Ban Treaty with Britain and America. Although this, in itself, could not signify an end to the cold War – Krushchev said, "You do not like our social system and we don't like yours. No treaties can overthrow the concrete contradictions between the two social systems" – and France refused to participate, it did at least give hope. It was also thought that Krushchev might have been speaking as much for the benefit of his home audience as anything. The loss of Krushchev raised the spectre of Russian isolation.

Below *President Kennedy with his brother, Robert (left)*

Right *Nina Krushchev views western fashion at the British Trade Fair in Moscow, 1961.*

Left and **opposite** *Disturbing images of Vietnam began to proliferate in the press in 1968, fanning the growing anti-war movement.*

Although a new, unknown Soviet leader was an anxiety, an even greater threat to the West now appeared to be China, which had broken off relations with the Soviet Union in 1959 and now appeared set on challenging the Soviets as leaders of the communist world. The breakdown in Sino-Soviet peace talks, which Krushchev personally boycotted, added a new dimension to international tension, particularly as China was already undertaking military action against India, stating that it was obliged to counter the nuclear threat of the USA.

A third event immediately preceding the election was the international recognition of the Civil Rights Movement when Martin Luther King was awarded the Nobel Peace Prize, in recognition of his doctrine of non-violence. This was in strong contrast with Goldwater's propaganda portraying the Civil Rights Movement as violent and subversive.

Johnson's inaugural address invoked the image of Kennedy. Not only did he refer back to the previous occasion when he had taken the Presidential oath on the plane bearing Kennedy's body, but he echoed Kennedy in his promise of "a great society" where there was to be "no domination over our fellow men but man's domination over tyranny and misery". Nevertheless, the civil rights situation in the South remained much as before. The beginning of 1965 saw King, despite his Nobel Peace Prize, once again jailed for protesting in Alabama against the slow implementation of the 1964 Civil Rights Act (only six percent of Alabama blacks were on the electoral register), and a month later, Johnson supplemented local police with FBI agents and three thousand troops to protect King and some 25,000 marchers presenting a petition to Governor Wallace in the capital of Alabama.

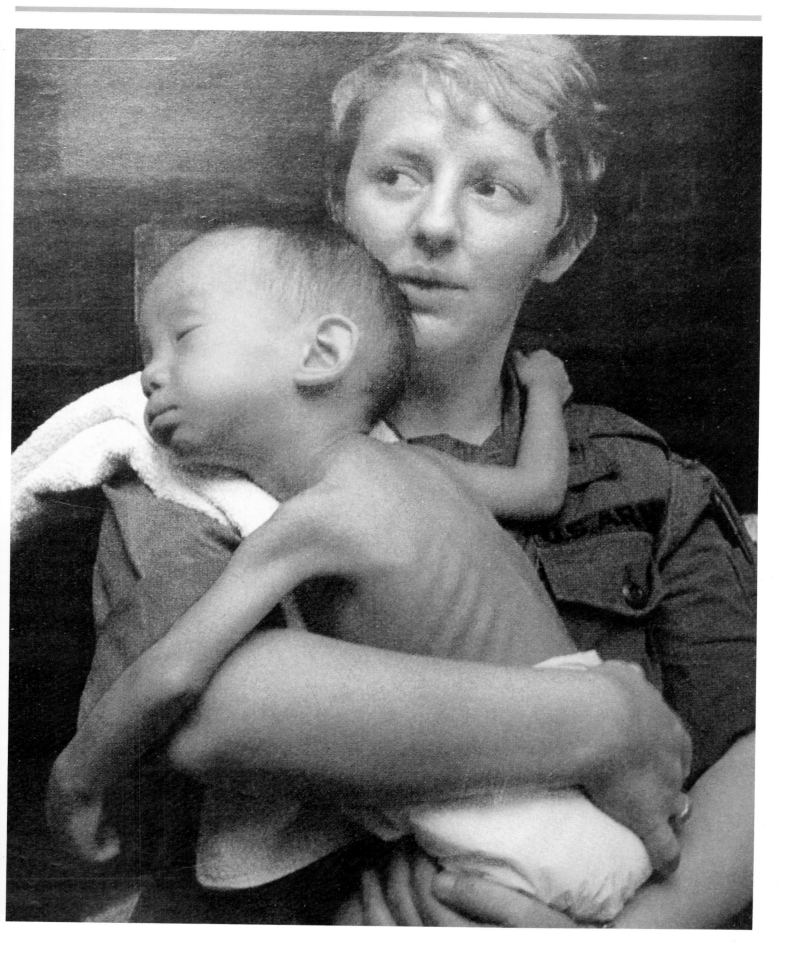

But now civil rights was no longer an exclusively Southern issue, nor was King's doctrine of non-violence any longer in control. At the same time as the Civil Rights Act was going through Congress, a new type of urban violence had arisen, in the form of three days of rioting in New York. National Guardsmen with armoured cars had battled with mobs hurling Molotov cocktails. Although Johnson had successfully repudiated Goldwater's portrayal of civil rights as synonymous with violence, the scene was repeated with greater intensity in, August 1965, when the black district of Los Angeles, Watts, erupted. Following the 'routine' arrest of a black for drunken driving, rioting, during which police and fire services were often under fire from rooftop snipers, claimed twenty eight lives and nearly a thousand injuries. Much of the district was set alight, with over a thousand fires, whilst looters took advantage of the confusion. When order was restored with the assistance of 20,000 National Guardsmen, over 2,000 looters had been arrested and total damage amounted to some $175 million. Designating Watts a disaster area, Johnson castigated the riot as a betrayal of the doctrine of non-violence, declaring that it "strikes from the hand of the negro the very weapons with which he is achieving his own emancipation".

By now, King's ethos of non-violence was becoming discredited within the Civil Rights Movement itself. In 1966 James Meredith, who had made history by being the first black student to be admitted to the University of Mississippi in 1962, was shot and wounded as he entered Mississippi on a civil rights march. He reacted with the statement: "The day for the negro man being a coward is over." In July three cities — Chicago, New York and Cleveland — saw violent riots. In Chicago, as in Watts, there was sniper fire against police, necessitating the moving in of four thousand National Guardsmen, whilst in New York one thousand extra police were called in as fighting broke out amongst the city's black and Hispanic population. Almost a year later, in the worst urban rioting to date, Detroit erupted to the extent that paratroopers had to be called in to assist the police and the National Guard restore order. In the course of the riot, some forty peope were shot.

Below *James Baldwin pictured during one of his tours of the South in 1963.*

With his civil rights policy now in pieces, Johnson was coming in for increasing criticism over the issue of Vietnam. Since 1965 the press had been giving greater coverage to the war, and from that time the anti-war movement at home, as well as foreign reaction, dogged the escalation which Johnson had hoped to keep secret. In 1966 8,000 American troops attacked a Vietcong centre known as the Iron Triangle. This was the first time the US had acted on is own initiative, rather than under the direction of South Vietnam, and marked the point of no return for American military commitment, confirming fears that had been voiced both at home and abroad, since the troops first went out. In the same year the first Australian troops joined the conflict and, for the first time, bombing raids were directed at Hanoi, drawing protests from the British Government. This was to be an unpopular war, weakening the status of the United States in world politics. At home not only did the ever-mounting toll of casualties have a demoralizing effect (in the words of a protest song: 'You can be the first on the block to have your kid come home in a box'), but the high financial cost eroded the domestic budget to the detriment of social programmes.

In 1966 television too began to give coverage, bringing the reality of war into homes in a way that was unprecedented. Not only was news film being shown uncensored but the reality of the horror was made still more vivid by the widespread accessibility of colour television in 1965 and 1966. In addition to American reportage, film from foreign sources also began to be shown. In 1967 CBS commissioned a documentary called *Inside North Vietnam* with the intention that, whilst it would provide material for news programmes, it would also show the effect of the war on ordinary Vietnamese.

Right *Many serving in Vietnam found their own values, cynical of the politics that had brought them there.*

Below *By 1966 Hanoi was claiming 1000 US planes downed (the Americans admitted to 257). Here North Vietnamese haul away the remains of one.*

Even more shocking, CBS TV's documentary *Morley Safer's Vietnam* of the same year, portrayed the American military not as fighters for peace and freedom but rather as callous killers. One sequence showed a helicopter crew being interviewed after a successful strike. First, the captain: "I feel real good when we do it . . .". Then the pilot explains, "I feel just like it's another target. You know, like in the States you shot at dummies, over here you shoot at Vietnamese Cong." Offscreen, a voice is heard admonishing the pilot over his terminology – "Cong, you shoot at Cong. You don't shoot at Vietnamese – and the pilot continues, "All right. You shoot at Cong. Anyway, when you come out on the run and then you see them an they come into your sights, it's just like a wooden dummy or something there, you just thumb off a couple pair of rockets. Like they weren't people at all." The human cost of the war was also being revealed. In 1967 one week alone saw one hundred and fifty American soldiers killed and over a thousand casualties. Amongst the young, protest demonstrations were taking place, as well as the passive protests of dropping out to San Francisco or the rural communes or fleeing the draft to Canada or Sweden. Refusing the draft in accordance with his black Muslim principles, Muhammad Ali, the former World Heavyweight Champion, Cassius Clay, voiced the opinon of many when he said, "I ain't got no quarrel with them Vietcongs."

Now vilified at home and abroad, his domestic civil rights policy and Vietnam foreign policy failing, Johnson had little to show for his Kennedy inheritance. Only six years before Kennedy had spoken of "the torch [being] passed to a new generation of Americans". Now, on every issue, America was more openly in revolt than ever before. In October a peaceful anti-war rally turned violent when it moved on to surround the Pentagon. The images of confrontation, with protestors, including Norman Mailer, facing an inscrutable rank of military

police, whose rifles pointed straight at them – in particular, Bernie Boston's photograph of a young protester inserting carnations in the guns' barrels – were seen all over the world, uniting local anti-war movements into an international force. Mailer was one of 250 people arrested at this protest. Many of the protesters were clubbed with truncheons and rifle butts. By December 1967 the anti-war movement was affecting the morale of the troops. Bob Hope, fulfilling the patriotic role he had taken on in the forties of entertaining the forces, gave a Christmas concert in Vietnam. In one sketch he appeared with Phil Cosby, both wearing long-haired wigs and carrying peace banners: "Don't worry about the riots

Above *In addition to the American defoliant programme, large areas were cleared for military use such as this landing strip.*

Left *Asked for their views on the presidential candidate, these soldiers backed Nixon ". . . He doesn't promise things you know can't be done, like bringing troops home in '69 . . .".*

Above *Despite the theatrical perfection of the gesture, the symbolic placing of flowers into the National Guardsmen's rifles was a real event.*

Opposite *American students display the Black Power clenched fist emblem during a protest in 1969.*

in the States, you'll be sent to survival school when you get there." That month, Ho Chi Minh sent New Year greetings to American peace groups.

The beginning of 1968 heralded a crisis year in American history. In Vietnam the bombing of South Vietnamese cities, which had been partially occupied by the Vietcong, was negating the original reason for the American presence, and General Westmoreland was asking Johnson for two hundred thousand more troops. Johnson's renomination was under threat from Robert Kennedy, who was now looking toward the Presidency, whilst Senator McCarthy announced that he would run against Johnson on a peace ticket. In March, following McCarthy's success in achieving forty percent of the vote against him in the New Hampshire primary and Kennedy's declaration of candidacy, Johnson unexpectedly finished a television broadcast on Viet-

nam with the announcement that he would not be seeking re-election. Although it was not known at the time, Richard Nixon, out of the public eye since his defeat by Kennedy, was about to step back on the political stage.

The preceding two years of mounting civil unrest had put an enormous strain on the Civil Rights Movement. Money earmarked for the social problem had long been lost to finance the war. Blacks were comparing their situation in Vietnam, where they were being asked to die for a country which still denied them full equality, with their lot at home, where poverty was driving more into the extremist camps. King posed the crucial question, "Why have we substituted the arrogant undertaking of policing the whole world for the high risk of puting our own house in order?" He was now in a dilemma, for a march was on the move to Washington.

Above *Seconds after the assassination of Martin Luther King, bystanders point to the source of the fatal shots.*

The mood had changed since 1963. The existence of militant factions and the city riots meant that the marchers would not be conditioned by the Church-led crusade of the South which had characterized the early Civil Rights Movement. King agonized as to whether or not to participate, finally being persuaded that his presence was essential to ensure its non-violence. On April 4th he was shot by a sniper. His death sparked off massive rioting in nearly all major cities, including Washington, where burning and looting took place only a few hundred yards from the White House. King's funeral was seen via satellite across the world, a moving event that temporarily united the country — if not politically at least by a shared sense of momentous tragedy. The assassination had the effect of giving momentum to Robert Kennedy's presidential campaign. In itself it represented the defeat of both his brother's and King's work. Determined that they should not have died in vain, he now seemed recklessly to disregard the niceties of political image, prominently including in his team civil rights activists. Following King's death, he conducted an almost evangelical campaign, then two months and a day later, he too was struck down by an assassin's bullet. As he fell, a bystander screamed, "Not again!" In the flurry of eulogies and laments, recriminations and explanations that followed, Arthur Schlesinger Jnr's comment found echoes in many Americans' hearts: "We are today the most frightening people on the planet."

Below *Although black and white anti-segregationalists were united at King's funeral, his death gave further ammunition to those who were turning against his creed of non-violence.*

Overleaf *With urban unrest on the increase, this 1967 chewing gum slogan was perhaps rather tasteless.*

CHAPTER SIX

THE RETURN OF NIXON

If, as it seemed, Kennedy and King were like figures from a Greek tragedy, the world's students were to be the chorus. In March London saw civil disorder when an estimated crowd of eighty thousand protested against the war in Vietnam outside the American Embassy. Although neither police nor protesters used serious weapons, there were severe injuries on both sides and three hundred arrests were made. In America the student occupation of Columbia University, in protest against the University's connection with the Defence Department via the Institute for Defence Analysis, resulted in the hospitalization of 77 students, 8 faculty members, 2 outsiders, 16 police and a total of 592 arrests.

In France, the conflict between an entrenched, insular and stultifying academic Establishment (summed up in the Nanterre graffiti 'Professors you are old and so is your culture') and a student body whose innate political awareness was reinforced by the large number of foreign students attending colleges, began to manifest itself in protests through 1966 and 1967 that would climax by bringing the country to the brink of Civil War in 1968.

Below *Richard Nixon with Checkers (right), the dog who made political history.*

Alongside specific grievances against the education system and de Gaulle's Government, protests against Vietnam and an affinity with international protest movements (particularly the German students' activities against the right-wing Springer newspaper group which led to the shooting of student leader Rudi Deutschke in April 1968) created an atmosphere of rebellion in the colleges. In February Nanterre University had been temporarily closed following the students' occupation of the administration building under the leadership of Daniel Cohn-Bendit (Danny the Red) and the Sorbonne was becoming the focal point for the student protest movement, with six students being arrested in March fol-

Below *The violent treatment student demonstrators received from the CRS created a wave of public sympathy.*

lowing an anti-Vietnam demonstration. Both the Government and the education authorities were by now determined to stem the flood of protest, though it is not known whether the repressive action which resulted in consolidating both student protest and general dissatisfaction into a challenge to the Government was deliberately provocative or merely mismanaged. On

Friday May 3rd a Sorbonne meeting to discuss the previous days re-closure of Nanterre was ended by the police, who, the University authorities claimed, had been called in to protect the students against a right-wing anti-protest group. The arrest of many students sparked off a riot during which students and sympathizers countered the police batons and tear gas by throwing paving stones; 72 police and an unknown number of protesters were injured, and six hundred arrested.

The feeling that the student movement was now in direct conflict with the Government fermented during the weekend, and on Monday 6th some twenty thousand demonstrators took to the streets in an initially peaceful march which deteriorated into some

Above *Street demonstrations and the violence which ensued became a daily event in Paris.*

sixteen hours of street fighting against the police and CRS (riot police). The following days saw further confrontations, culminating in the night of the 10th, when from behind barricades built to defend the 'occupied' streets around the Sorbonne, protesters, now protecting themselves by wearing motorcycle helmets and masks soaked in lemon juice to counter gas, fought the police with paving stones and Molotov cocktails. By now revulsion at the sight of police brutality was attracting public support, and the trade union movement endorsed a protest strike for May 13th. Although this was intended only as an official protest, the mood of rebellion which had permeated much of French Society resulted in unofficial action, so that by the 16th some fifty factories were occupied by their workers. On the 18th the trade unions, with some two hundred thousand people, including white collar workers now on strike, called for a general strike. On the 23rd, with over nine million strikers, France was effectively in a state of civil rebellion. De Gaulle made an ineffective televised appeal for peace on the 24th, and in the night of rioting that followed a mob attacked and set fire to the Paris Stock Exchange (the Bourse), whilst elsewhere the first officially acknowledged death occurred when a young man was killed by a grenade. It seemed that the commonly-voiced rumour that the de Gaulle Government would be toppled might become a reality. Nevertheless, having secretly secured the support of the right wing element of the Army, De Gaulle was confident enough to make a short radio announcement on May 30th in which he dissolved Parliament pending new elections, stated his refusal to resign and gave the country the alternatives of returning to work or facing the consequences of his calling a State of Emergency. A stage-managed pro de Gaulle demonstration of some eight hundred thousand people brought in from all over France marched in Paris and, with the encouragement of the unions, many strikes were called off

Amongst those that held out were the Renault and Peugeot factories which were occupied by students and workers. A young student died on June 10 in the aftermath of the four-day battle during which the CRS ejected the protesters from Renault, and the next day two workers were killed when the CRS fired shots at the Peugeot strikers. The student leaders, faced with several of their organisations by now being declared illegal, and the reality that not only would continual confrontation result in further deaths, but de Gaulle's calling of an election meant that many of their supporters were looking forward to a democratic solution, stopped organising demonstrations, and on 16 June, with only token opposton, the police cleared the Sorbonne and surrouding streets of students. The end of the month saw the success of de Gaulle's propaganda claim that the whole episode had been a communist plot in his triumphant re-election with an even bigger majority than before!

Opposite *In France revolutionary posters proliferated as a form of protest folk art.*

Below *CRS police by an abandoned barricade. The pile of paving stones had been prepared as missiles.*

Left *The British would-be revolutionaries aped the French style of protest graphics.*

Above *Grosvenor Square, site of the American Embassy in London, became the scene for anti-Vietnam demonstrations and the inevitable confrontation with the police.*

As well as the anti-Vietnam demonstrations, Britain, too, had its protest movement. In 1967 the London School of Economics had been occupied by over one thousand students, thirteen of whom had carried out a five day hunger strike in protest against the appointment of a new Director who had formerly been head of University College, Rhodesia. The occupation, or sit-in, became a feature of academic life as protests against a variety of causes were registered. In May 1968 the students of Hornsey College of Art occupied the main college building in protest against the administration of the college and the state of art education in general. Joined by some of the teaching staff, who shared the students' lack of identity and sense of purpose, the occupiers utilized the college facilites to put out a series of manifestos, the products of the peace of mind which can be enjoyed by revolutionaries safe in the knowledge that they would never be called on to face bullets or tear gas. Most of the British college protests ended to coincide with the beginning of the summer recess and, by the start of the new academic year, the protest movement was virtually over. In October a demonstration by some quarter of a million anti-war protesters outside the American embassy was notable for its lack of violent incidents.

In America, however, the violence continued. There was even an attempt on the life of Andy Warhol, who was shot by a member of SCUM (Society for Cutting Up Men, a militant feminist group). With Kennedy dead, the liberal camp was in the hands of McCarthy who, in contrast to Kennedy, avoided emotion in favour of a detached, academic and sometimes even mystical approach. He had an ability to make controversial statements as though they were self-evident truths which did not need any embellishment. One such was his statement on television that the fifties and sixties had been characterized by judging the political systems of other nations of the world, accepting that we had the right to interfere with all those systems if we found them wanting – which condemned by implication Kennedy's foreign policy, which Johnson had inherited. Nixon

was now the Republican nominee and, although McCarthy gained the suport of the Peace Movement, his rejection of the Kennedy-Johnson foreign policy alienated many Democrats, who wished for a vindication of those years. Their preferred candidate was Hubert Humphrey. The Democrats' Convention in Chicago would thus be seen as the test of two ideologies, with Nixon able to sit back, innocent of any responsibility for the events of the decade.

With Johnson – and by implication his natural successor, Humphrey – branded a warmonger, Chicago was prepared for confrontation. Unfortunately, under the enthusiastic direction of Mayor Richard Daley, it was over-prepared. Barbed-wire fences surrounded the Convention centre and police were instructed in riot control. Although only a relatively small num-

ber – some 10,000 – demonstrators went to lobby the Convention, including a civil rights group led by King's successor, Ralph Abernathy and peace protesters, the efforts of Daley to keep demonstrators clear of the Convention area, as well as the formidable array of police, created a climate in which confrontation was inevitable. Protestors trying to get near the Convention area were faced with police armed with nightsticks, guns and tear gas, backed up by National Guardsmen.

Below *Senator Hubert Humphrey extends the hand of electioneering bonhomie in 1960.*

Right Enfant terrible *of sixties art, Andy Warhol, survived an assassination attempt by a militant feminist.*

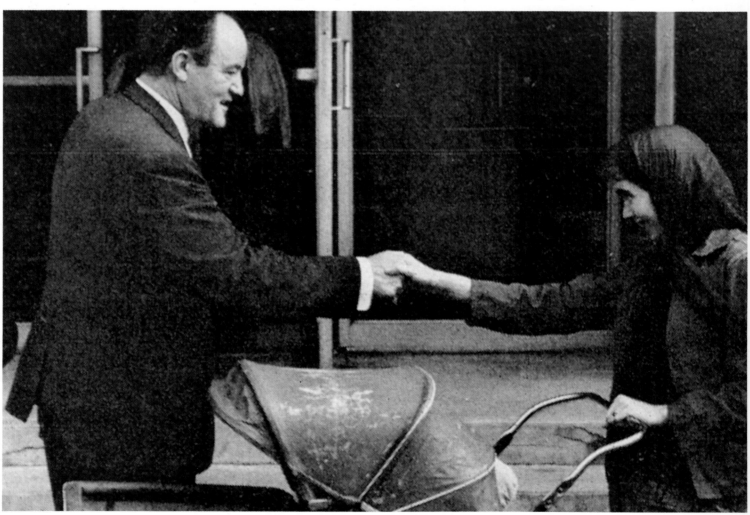

Not content with attacking the protestors in full view of television cameras and the world's press, police even entered the Convention and dragged two delegates from the hall, bringing protests against the 'Gestapo tactics' of Daley's force. Amongst those injured were twenty-one reporters and cameramen, clubbed by the police for recording these extraordinary events. The debacle of the Democrats' Convention resulted in the nomination of Humphrey and the defeat of an anti-war motion. On November 6th Richard Nixon beat Humphrey in an election which was characterized by a low electoral turnout, a reflection of the low esteem in which politics were now held. In one of his last acts as President, Johnson ordered a total halt to the bombing of North Vietnam, in exchange for which the North Vietnamese agreed to South Vietnam being represented at the Paris peace talks.

Within weeks of becoming President, Nixon not only secretly resumed the bombing, but also ordered the bombing of Cambodia, a neutral country. Just as Goldwater had distracted attention from Johnson's aggressive policy in Vietnam, so, in turn, Nixon was benefiting from his public image as a dove. Whilst the war effort was secretly escalating, the public were told that the war was winding down, with television coverage of returning troops reinforcing the official slogan 'we are on our way out of Vietnam'. Within a few months the truth about Cambodia was exposed by the New York Times and, in full knowledge of the escalation, the Peace Movement resumed its protest with renewed vigour. John Lennon and his wife Yoko Ono, turned their honeymoon into a 'bed-in' for peace. Surrounded by the world's press, the couple sat in bed for a week to draw attention to the war, a safe form of protest with no risk of bloodied heads, but an endorsement both of the comfort of the presidential suite of the Amsterdam Hilton, the venue of this protest, and the couple's considerable egos.

Above *The 1968 Democratic Party Convention degenerated into violent mayhem.*

With consummate political skill, Nixon (the Great Communicator) went on television on November 3rd and, with an audience in excess of 70 million viewers, appealed to the 'silent majority'. His appeal to the patriotism of 'fellow Americans' made the point that an America seen abroad as divided was thus weakened in peace negotiations, as well as painting an emotive picture of the humiliation of defeat: "North Vietnam cannot defeat or humiliate the United States. Only Americans can do that." This speech evoked Kennedy's image of an America united by a common goal, and had the effect of temporarily turning public opinion against the Peace Movement. The silent majority, in any event, was by now tired of the decade of protest. In the Spring of 1969, Berkeley had been the scene of the most violently suppressed student protest, although the next year Kent State would surpass that dubious achievement. Initially organized by San Francisco hippies, but quickly endorsed by the students, the Berkeley protest was over the issue of whether some university land should be used, as the authorities wanted, for sports fields or dormitory buildings, or, as the hippies wanted, for a 'political freak-out and rap centre'. Unprecedented counter-action included not only the presence of the National Guard but also the spraying of tear gas from a police helicopter. The 'Battle for People's Park' on May 15th resulted in injuries to both police and protesters, one death, forty-three proetesters receiving bullet wounds and nearly a thousand arrests.

Right *At Berkeley University in 1968 heavily-armed National Guardsmen faced passive protesters.*

Black civil rights was now also firmly linked in the public mind with violence. Students, both white and black, were demanding academic recognition of Black Studies and, in an ironic reversal of the de-segregation demands of the original civil liberties movement, exclusively black colleges. Cornell University was occupied by protestors demanding black separatism. When the occupiers peacefully vacated a college hall they had occupied, it was discovered that they had had seventeen rifles and shotguns in the building.

By now there was a backlash against protest. Whilst Berkeley was again in the news – a seven week strike in support of the Third World Liberation Front and the Afro-American student union – Governor Ronald Reagan kept a permanent force of one thousand National Guardsmen in readiness for any confrontation, and at the University of Wisconsin nearly two thousand National Guardsmen were called into escort white students barred from classes by the Black People's Alliance. It seemed a return to the days of Wallace and Alabama: only the colour had changed. The silent majority watched these events, backed Nixon and hoped that the last decade had just been a bad dream.

Below *Afro-American students who had been occupying a hall at Cornell University leave, still bearing the weapons they had brought to defend themselves.*

Right *As Governor of California, Ronald Reagan's original liberal image was soon tarnished when he put the National Guard on permanent alert to counter protests.*

INDEX